THE WOMAN'S GUIDE TO
TOTAL
SELF-ESTEEM

THE EIGHT SECRETS YOU NEED TO KNOW

STEPHANIE DILLON, PH.D.

FOREWORD BY M. CHRISTINA BENSON, M.D.

NEW HARBINGER PUBLICATIONS, INC.

D0150260

Publisher's Note

Distributed in Canada by Raincoast Books

Copyright © 2001 by Stephanie Dillon and M. Christina Benson
New Harbinger Publications, Inc.
5674 Shattuck Avenue
Oakland, CA 94609

Cover design by Blue Designs
Cover photo by Digital Imagery © 2001 PhotoDisc, Inc.
Edited by Brady Kahn
Text design by Spencer Smith

ISBN-10 1-57224-241-8
ISBN-13 978-1-57224-241-8

FSC
Mixed Sources
Product group from well-managed
forests and other controlled sources

Cert no. SW-COC-002283
www.fsc.org
© 1996 Forest Stewardship Council

Printed in the United States of America

New Harbinger Publications' website address: www.newharbinger.com

11   10   09

10   9   8   7   6   5

Contents

Preface

We write this book for all women who are struggling to cope with busy, demanding lives and whose low self-esteem is making life even harder. We write this book for women of every age and description, for working mothers, single women, married women, stay-at-home wives, career women, women on welfare, lesbian women, bisexual women, straight women, celibate women, old women, young women, women in mid-life. We write this book for women who have not had the support, understanding, and tools to create good and enduring self-esteem. We also write this book for women who have good self-esteem and who need extra help at times of stress when their self-esteem is low. That means almost all of us, at least some of the time.

We also write this book for men who are struggling to better understand the women in their lives. We write this book for men who are confused about why their wives, sisters, girlfriends, and daughters are often so harsh and self-critical about their bodies, their accomplishments, and themselves. We write this book for men who want to know more about why the women who are most important to them can function in a balanced way, and then, out of nowhere, explode into angry blaming outbursts or slide into deep depression. Through a greater understanding of women's difficulties, men will have more compassion for women who are trying their best.

All men have an overt or covert "feminine" side, just as all women have an overt or covert "masculine" side. We write this book for men who are interested in understanding more about their own struggle to better integrate the masculine and feminine within themselves.

This book evolved from our clinical work as well as our personal experience. Every woman we have known struggles with valuing herself sufficiently and staying true to those values. From accomplished M.D.s to intelligent women with a fifth-grade education, self-esteem remains a battle.

We offer this book to women as a blueprint for enhancing their self-esteem. Using the concepts and techniques in this book, women will hopefully discover deep within themselves a woman with a stronger spirit and a truer sense of who she is.

Acknowledgments

I want to thank M. Christina Benson, M.D., for adding conceptual depth and richness to this book. I also want to thank her for her faith in me and in this project.

For their unique and important contributions to this book I want to thank Luanne Oakes, Judy Phoenix, Andrew Crane, Elizabeth Pomada, George Mannen, Ken Wells, Karen Jacobs, Brent Begley, Mike and Barbara Land, Dawn Lee Lipschutz-Snell, Betty Manning, Warren Goedert, Steve Graybar, Mike Larsen, Catherine Blake and the women of Ridge House, Ella W. Dillon and James Edward Dillon, Sr., Mildred Maxfield, David Kent, Catharine Sutker, Lilah Dillon and especially, Stevie and Duke.

Introduction

Women are traditionally trained to be caring and compassionate, sensitive and responsive to the needs of others. Our world consists in large part of doing things for our husbands, children, parents, friends, community, bosses, brothers, uncles, aunts, co-workers, and we often find significant meaning and satisfaction for ourselves along the way. But we also confront the danger of losing or never discovering our real selves.

Culture and history tell us that we should value ourselves through our relationships. We have been taught through the ages that in order to get our needs met we must follow a societal feminine script, one that requires that we put the needs of others before our own. We must sacrifice ourselves on the altar of caring for others. A "good" mother puts the needs of her children before her own.

It may be appropriate in many situations for a mother to put her child's needs ahead of her own. However, a mother's ability to nurture effectively over time depends upon her willingness to engage in consistent self-care so that she operates from a well of energy that is more full than empty. Trying to nourish others from a consistently depleted self eventually leads to an impoverished quality of nurturing.

Many of us believe that if we follow the feminine script we will be loved. If we don't feel loved, we will often do more to try to get our needs met: more caregiving, more cooking, more staying up late to get everything done, and, in the worst cases, more forgiving of the unforgivable: abuse. Often, in an attempt to be loved and recognized, acknowledged and appreciated, we keep increasing our attempts to do more to please bosses, husbands, children, friends. If we still don't feel loved and appreciated, we may become ill, get depressed, feel helpless and hopeless, or even lash out in anger and frustration.

Gender Prison

Men and women both suffer from being handed a historical cultural script. Following this script in order to be acknowledged, appreciated, and valued creates a situation in which both men and women are sentenced to an indeterminate time in gender prison.

The Script for Women

According to the feminine script, women are supposed to be empathic, caring, warm, nurturing, patient, sensitive but not too sensitive, long-suffering, intuitive, selfless, tender, forgiving, trusting—almost a Christ-like job description.

If we get angry, we risk being labeled a "bitch" or at least "bitchy." We are encouraged to not make scenes, to keep quiet, even when we are treated with disrespect, but simultaneously we are expected to stand up for others (children, family, friends, and even strangers unable to help themselves) and assist others in getting their needs met.

We are trained to get our sense of worth and value from our relationships—from what we do for others and how we make others feel important and special. Hence, many of us believe that if we just follow the script and act "feminine," we will be loved and valued.

The Script for Men

According to the masculine script, men are supposed to be aggressive, competitive, objective, controlled, rational, unemotional, strong, powerful, invulnerable, skeptical, tough. Men are encouraged to speak up when they are not treated with respect. Men are taught to stand up for themselves and to protect those less powerful. Men are told not to cry, but that it's okay to be angry.

Men are taught to get their self-esteem from what they do and achieve in the world. Men are taught that if they follow their script, they will be admired—even envied—valued, and recognized.

How We Learn the Script

The feminine script is taught early in life and is powerfully reinforced as girls grow into women.

Research on gender-role stereotypes began to increase in the 1950s. Parson and Bales (1955) found that society associates masculinity with problem-solving and instrumental actions, and femininity with expressing oneself emotionally, being concerned for others, and placing a high value on cooperation, rather than competition. Later studies showed that masculinity is associated with a concern for oneself and femininity with a concern for the relationship between oneself and others (Bakan 1996).

It has been documented that the differential treatment of males and females begins when the gender of a child is discovered (Sidorowicz and Lunney 1980), and that parents describe their newborn's physical attributes and personality in gender-stereotyped ways (Rubin, Provenzano, and Luria 1974).

The expectations others have about appropriate gender behavior leads children to internalize the expectations contained within the masculine and feminine scripts.

Gender-role behaviors are taught, often unconsciously, by parents and teachers, peers and culture, especially the media (Etaugh and Liss 1992; Liss 1983). As children move through early and mid childhood and into late childhood, they become more stringent enforcers of gender-role stereotyped behavior in themselves and others (Fagot 1977; Fagot and Patterson 1969; Lamb and Roopnarine 1979). Burford and Foley (1996) effectively summarized extensive research in the area of sex-role stereotypes.

The Dangers Inherent in the Scripts

The scripts that men and women have been trained to follow exist to some degree in all of us. They influence how we perceive and value ourselves and others. We have internalized the scripts for so long, they are often hidden from our conscious awareness. These internalized scripts diminish and devalue women and men. The scripts obscure our similarities and emphasize our differences, which creates unnecessary divisiveness and disharmony, leaving us less able to connect with and learn from the experience of the other gender.

The scripts limit the ability of all of us to know and claim our unique selves. A man may feel sad when his mother is ill, but he is not supposed to cry. A woman may feel angry and insulted when a colleague comes on to her, but she isn't supposed to show it.

The feminine script is damaging to the self-esteem of girls and women because both males and females in our culture place a positive value on masculine characteristics and devalue feminine characteristics (Friedan 1963, 1984). Our culture idealizes characteristics considered to be masculine: self-reliance, independence, athleticism, assertiveness, strong personality, forcefulness, analytic ability, leadership abilities, risk-taking, quick decision-making, self-sufficiency, dominance, aggressiveness. Our culture denigrates characteristics considered feminine: being yielding, cheerful, shy, affectionate, susceptible to flattery, sympathetic, sensitive, understanding, compassionate, and of comfort to others (Kelly, Candill, Hathorn, and O'Brien 1977).

Following the feminine script leads to low self-esteem. The differential valuing of masculine and feminine characteristics is reflected in the workplace. Thirty years after the feminist revolution, in spite of comprising more than half of the workforce, women make 71 cents for every dollar that men make (Friedan 1997). Women are overrepresented in some professions (teaching, childcare, direct human services) and underrepresented in high-dollar power positions (corporate heads, political offices).

As long as the women's training program and the feminine script remain outside of our conscious awareness, we will not be able to fully be who we really are.

Beliefs That Shape Us

Cultural and historical beliefs shape how we see ourselves as women and how we are seen. These beliefs can be encouraging and empowering of selfhood, as well as destructive and limiting. We need to develop clarity about the beliefs that determine how we perceive ourselves and are perceived. Only then will we be able to rewrite our scripts in a way that is more supportive and empowering.

The Belief That Women Must Find Meaning Through Attachments

As girls and women, we are taught to find our meaning and worth through our attachments to others. We are blessed, as well as cursed, with relatedness to others: girlfriends, husbands, children, family, community.

The good news is that our gift of deep relatedness is a humanizing and absolutely essential ingredient of any world worth living in. The bad news is that too much relatedness, without a sturdy real self, becomes empty and crippling. A self defined only by relatedness to others may become the object of our own deep resentment and rage, creating a world that is unbearable.

The Belief That Our Superficial Characteristics Must Define And Limit Who We Are

We are defined by how we look, by how closely we approximate the cultural standard of beauty. That standard is an arbitrary and artificial belief, but one that we internalize and then apply to ourselves. How well we succeed or fail is an accident of birth. If you were a woman in 1750, you needed to look Reubenesque, amply endowed and curvaceous.

In 1920s America, the flapper was the idol: thin, small-breasted, straight up and down. In the 1950s it was better to be Marilyn, blonde and busty, or Sophia, dark and voluptuous. In the late 1960s, Twiggy was it—thin was in. In the early '90s, Kate Moss was the icon, followed by tall, thin, big-breasted blondes. Many of us despise our perfectly good bodies because we don't meet the current cultural standards of beauty. The increase in eating disorders is testimony to the damage done by these capricious standards of how women should look. Some women exercise while injured, starve, or binge and purge to try to meet the cultural standards of the moment. Others of us have injured ourselves emotionally, putting ourselves down because we don't attain the cultural standard for how women are supposed to be (married with children, blessed with the perfect body).

Ageism

As men age, they are often seen as more distinguished, more experienced, wiser. As women age, they are often seen as dried out old bags, no longer desirable. Ageism places a premium on what's on the outside for women, neglecting the person-specific qualities that characterize a particular woman. We can no longer afford to be unaware of the toll that ageism takes on the self-esteem of all women.

Sexism

As a recent American Association of University Women (1992) study documented, things are very much the same in the classroom as they were decades ago. Girls' academic achievements are still overlooked. The study of kindergartener through twelfth graders shows that boys receive about five times more attention from teachers than girls; boys also speak up in the classroom twelve times more than girls. Boys are praised for giving a correct answer; girls are praised for how they give an answer (politely, sweetly, and nicely), or how they look.

Teachers respond differently to boys and girls, just because of their gender. "The message to boys tends to be: 'You're smart, if you would just settle down and get to work.' The message to girls is often: 'Perhaps you're just not good at this. You've followed the rules and haven't succeeded'" (Pipher 1994, 62–63). Teachers have internalized the masculine and feminine scripts and unconsciously reinforce sex-role stereotypes by rewarding boys and girls according to the gender-appropriate rules. Hundreds of adolescent girls have told us that they don't participate in class because of their anxiety about being perceived as too smart—not feminine. High school girls have told us they often meet at lunch or after school with teachers to learn as much as they can without the social stigma of speaking up in class.

In the worlds of business and academia, there have been some improvements: more women are functioning in professional positions. Some gains have been made. Still, women do not have economic parity or equal social and political power. Even successful women and sensitive men have been unable to adequately humanize the workplace or politics, the seats of power.

Masculine and Feminine

Across time, masculine has come to stand for doing, acting, and making things happen in the world. Men move things along with goals: financial, social, and political outcomes. The feminine has come to stand for nurturing, compassion, and empathy; for service on behalf of relationships. The truth is, the masculine and the feminine exist sometimes as allies, sometimes as enemies, in each of us, regardless of gender.

All of us, male and female, need to create a better balance of the masculine and the feminine within us. This is the path to a more integrated self, more connected relationships, and a better world.

Self-Objectivity

For us as women, it is critically important to begin to look at ourselves realistically. Why are we like this? Why do we follow the feminine script until we can't stand it anymore and fall apart? Why is our choice only between following the feminine script or feeling that we are not worthy?

Each of us answers the question in her own way: "Because people expect too much of me." "Because I married the wrong man." "Because no one else at the office will work as hard as I do." "Because no one will love me or want me if I am truly myself." "Because I have low self-esteem." "Because I'm too fat, old, dumpy, ugly."

The struggle to find and maintain a true vibrant self and not retreat into a Barbiesque parody of the feminine script is a struggle for most women. This struggle is not an individual problem, and not even a generational problem. All of us are handed the same cultural and historical beliefs that guide us behaviorally and emotionally, even when we reject them intellectually.

Why We Wrote This Book

Through our clinical work with thousands of women clients, we have discovered how important self-esteem is to every area of a woman's life: her view of herself, her functioning at work, in relationships, as a mother and a wife.

This book came out of our role as therapists working with women clients, who have shown us that following the feminine script can lead to depression, anxiety, and confusion. Learning about the feminine script has helped these women master the objectivity they needed to begin to write their own scripts. Haltingly at first, and then more and more sure of themselves, they moved forward. They learned how to turn down the volume of the internal critic and give themselves credit. They learned how to accept their own unique bodies. They learned that the wild intuitive woman within is often the best guide to a new job or a new relationship. They learned how to edit and rewrite the old feminine script to suit their own particular needs and dreams.

Our woman clients have helped us get a better purchase on the complex layering of self-esteem, and now we want to pass this knowledge on to you. As you read this book, you'll find a number of stories about women who've worked on their self-esteem and gotten results. Though we've changes names and individual details, these stories are all based on the histories of other women like you. Read their stories and be inspired.

The Two Most Limiting Beliefs for Women

1. "If I am fully myself, no one will like me or want me."

2. "Men are powerful, women are weak."

Whether or not we are aware of it, all of us have been exposed to such limiting beliefs, and to some degree have used them to shape our sense of ourselves. We need to put some distance between ourselves and cultural prescriptions that don't or ought not to apply to us.

Read the two limiting beliefs above. Ask yourself, "How much do I believe this?" Then ask yourself, "Do I behave as if I believed this?" You may have been taught to accept certain ideas on faith. Now is the time to look at such beliefs critically in order to support the development of your unique self.

CHAPTER 1

The Power of Self-Esteem

Self-esteem critically affects how you function in your world. People with good self-esteem have more vitality and get more satisfaction out of their relationships and their jobs (Hardin 1999). Good self-esteem is the most crucial ingredient of mental health and well-being (Bednar, Wells, and Peterson 1989). Low self-esteem is associated with mental illness and poor life adjustment (Coopersmith 1967). It has also been determined that self-esteem is not a result of your social class, your father's occupation, your family wealth, your education, where you live, or whether you had a stay-at-home mom (Briggs 1977).

From research, we know that self-esteem is a multi-determined interaction of many influences. Factors such as family wealth, education, and social class are no guarantee that you will have good self-esteem. You can have millions of dollars and be perceived by others as "having it all," and yet feel empty and lonely deep inside, hiding your low self-esteem behind money and power. The self-esteem equation can also work in the other direction: you can have good self-esteem without wealth or high visibility.

Your self-esteem determines how you feel about yourself and your life. At the same time, the most important factor in determining your self-esteem as an adult is your commitment to improve it. With accurate knowledge of the components of self-esteem and the right techniques for change, you can be the architect of your own good self-esteem. Your investment in improving your own self-esteem will bring you wonderful rewards: greater satisfaction with yourself and your life, increased peace of mind, time for yourself every day without guilt, greater pleasure in work, play, and relationships, more ability to be in the moment, more passion, more power, and more freedom.

The Importance of Self-Esteem

Self-esteem has been the subject of thousands of books, articles, seminars, and workshops. The California Task Force on Self-Esteem has been in place since 1986. The International Congress on Self-Esteem meets yearly. Self-esteem is now considered the most significant determinant of a life well-lived (Briggs 1970; Branden 1994; Mruk 1995).

Researchers and theorists (Mruk 1995) have said that self-esteem is a complex blend of *competence* (your ability to learn specific skills that lead to mastery in any area of functioning) and *worthiness* (the actual value you place on yourself). In the self-esteem equation, the attainment of competence is emphasized for boys, whereas worthiness is emphasized for girls (Mruk 1995). Worthiness is mediated by relationships—how others perceive your value. If you are a girl, you have to figure out how others perceive you, i.e., whether you're okay in their eyes. Girls do this through hyper-vigilant attunement to the nuances of interpersonal feedback. If you are a boy, competence is mediated by performance—you win the soccer game, or you lose; you give the right or wrong answer.

This differential equation for self-esteem (boys are more rewarded for competence, girls more for pleasing others) results in girls trying to obtain self-esteem through their relationships. In high school basketball, for example, boys are encouraged to win, whatever it takes. Girls have the additional burden of wondering if they were cooperative enough, if they gave their teammates enough support, if their superior performance might lead to envy or even ostracism.

Defining Total Self-Esteem

Your *total self-esteem* is the combination of how you perceive yourself and the value you place on the multi-dimensional self you see. In order to have good self-esteem, you have to be able to assess your strengths and weaknesses objectively, without expecting yourself to be perfect.

For example, you may perceive yourself to be aggressive, stubborn, humorous, vulnerable, extroverted, sensitive, loud, and skinny.

You may have mixed feelings about being humorous, mildly negative feelings about being vulnerable, positive feelings about being extroverted, extremely positive feelings about being sensitive, and extremely negative feelings about being loud and skinny. How you value yourself in these areas may be conscious or unconscious, or a combination of the two.

Cognitive-Behavioral Approaches to Self-Esteem

Cognitive-behavioral approaches to changing human behavior stress that your sense of self-esteem is a result of how you think (McKay and Fanning 2000). Cognitive-behaviorists focus on assisting clients to recognize and change patterns of negative thinking about themselves. This approach has made a significant contribution in helping us recognize how negative thinking patterns can damage self-esteem.

Cognitive-behaviorists assume that thoughts cause feelings: "I think, therefore I feel." They would say that how you think about yourself is what determines your self-esteem.

The Missing Ingredient

The problem with cognitive-behavioral approaches is that they actually leave out a critical component of your self-esteem: the power of your feelings and emotions. In fact, self-esteem is a product of what you believe about yourself, and what you believe about yourself is determined both by how you think *and* how you feel about yourself. If you believe (think and feel) you are worthy and competent, there is a great probability that you will have good self-esteem. If you only think (but don't feel) that you are worthy and competent, your self-esteem is built on a shaky foundation.

Why We Avoid Putting Feelings Into the Self-Esteem Equation

We humans like to think of ourselves as different from other primates because of our superbly developed cerebral cortex and our resulting strengths in thinking. It is humbling for us to admit that our limbic system and the parts of the "old brain" that process feelings within milliseconds may be primary in our ability to survive and do well in life. Yet research has shown that emotions and feelings are a critical source of information in dealing successfully with life (Ekman 1994; Goleman 1995).

Think about the significant role that feelings have played in your life. Think about falling in love or making a decision to take a job that turned out to be fabulous, over a job that looked better on paper, and afterwards learning that the company where you turned down the job just went bankrupt. Though hard to pinpoint, perhaps, something in the job interview had made you skeptical. Think about the young man you turned down for a date who didn't want to take "no" for an answer. You turned him down because you had a gut feeling that something was wrong with him, and you were right. Think of all the times you have followed your intuition and been rewarded. Think about all the times you ignored your gut feeling and were disappointed and dismayed by the results.

It is not only true that thoughts cause feelings. "Because emotions can occur with a very rapid onset, through automatic appraisal, with little [cognitive or intellectual] awareness, and with involuntary changes in expression and physiology . . . we often experience emotions as happening to us, not as chosen by us" (Ekman 1994, 17).

In regard to human functioning and self-esteem, it would be more accurate to say, "I think and feel, therefore I am." Feelings and emotions interact with thinking to influence your self-esteem.

Total Self-Esteem

Total self-esteem is how you value your whole self, based on your ability to accurately assess your specific strengths. This includes your perceptions of and feelings about qualities and characteristics of yourself in several arenas: your physical self, your emotional, intellectual, and spiritual selves, and your self in relation to others. In the upcoming chapters we will focus on eight key areas in which your sense of self-esteem may be low, and help you work on:

- Developing Healthy Selfishness (chapter 2)

- Accepting Your Body When You Really Hate It (chapter 3)

- Acquiring the Courage to Feel (chapter 4)

- Getting Off the Emotional Tightrope (chapter 5)

- Facing the Mirror On the Wall (chapter 6)

- Rocketing Your Way to Self-Advocacy (chapter 7)

- Working on People Skills, Not People-Pleasing (chapter 8)

- Becoming the Parent You Always Wanted (chapter 9)

Each of these "eight secrets" to self-esteem is a collection of specific skills to be practiced and learned. For example, in "Getting Off the Emotional Tightrope," you will learn how to calm yourself when you are overwhelmed with intense feelings and how to motivate yourself when you feel unable to move forward. In "Facing the Mirror On the Wall," you will learn how to take credit for strengths that you overlook and to identify weaknesses in a nonjudgmental way. In "Accepting Your Body When You Really Hate It," you will learn why you have such a conflicted relationship with your body and how to make your body your ally, not your enemy.

Developing and maintaining good total self-esteem can be a life-long process. Enhancing your self-esteem requires learning how to take credit where credit is due and courageously overcome your own tendencies to undermine your self-esteem by being overly harsh and self-critical.

Again, your total self-esteem reflects both how you see yourself (overweight, intelligent, funny) and how you feel about the self you see (critical about being overweight, ambivalent about being intelligent, proud of your sense of humor). Your total self-esteem has been created by your genetic strengths and weaknesses interacting with the particular situation in which you grew up and with your life experience. Your total self-esteem is also an interactive process in which you respond to those in your world and those in your world impact you.

You carry this sense of total self-esteem with you into every life experience. You affect your world and the people in it, just as they affect you. Your total self-esteem continues to develop in every interaction between you and your world, throughout your life. Like most women, you may not have the objectivity that would be most helpful in accurately assessing the qualities that make up your unique individual self. Most women minimize their strengths and exaggerate their weaknesses, which results in a devalued sense of self. Most of us put too much emphasis on how we think others see us and not enough value on how we experience ourselves. Read the following story about a woman named Eleanor and compare her story with your own.

Eleanor's Story

Eleanor was the one everyone counted on. If the homeroom mother got sick, Eleanor stayed up until two in the morning and baked the class cupcakes. If her boss had to work over the weekend to make a deadline, Eleanor would be there to help, doing triple duty when she got home to feed her husband and children, do laundry, and clean the house. Sick neighbors, her crotchety mother-in-law, friends in romantic crisis, all could rely on Eleanor to meet their needs. Eleanor was able to show up and help for years. In her late thirties, Eleanor started having problems with loss of energy and increasing bouts of flu and colds. She found herself taking more sick days at work. Eleanor's boss finally confronted her. "I'm concerned about how you're doing. You're missing work more and more of the time. You don't have the same enthusiasm for the projects we're working on. What's going on?"

Eleanor decided to take a good look at her life. The things she loved to do, painting, fixing up castoffs from garage sales, walks with friends, reading before she went to bed, all these small pleasures had disappeared in the service of serving others. Eleanor realized that she had been feeling more and more depressed and overwhelmed. She felt that she had lost the very things that had nourished her and allowed her to give so much to others.

Eleanor looked deeply into herself and realized she needed to change some things about how she was operating in her life. She started a self-esteem journal which allowed her to plan time for herself each day and to take credit for caring for herself. She decided that she would claim forty-five minutes every day for herself, to use in any way she desired, even if the laundry didn't get done exactly on time.

After making her decision to care for herself on a daily basis, Eleanor felt relieved. Within a few months she had recaptured her verve, her vitality, and her enthusiasm for work, play, her family and friends.

Exercise: Your Self-Esteem Journal

The first step in improving your self-esteem is to start a self-esteem journal. The purpose of keeping a self-esteem journal is to help you plan time for yourself each day and take credit for the time you spend on yourself each day. Your self-esteem journal will help you to be scrupulously honest about exactly how much time you are investing in your own care and maintenance. The additional benefit of your self-esteem journal is that it will allow you to take credit for what you do for yourself. You may regularly put your own needs on the back burner, yet not be aware of how little time you give to yourself. The self-esteem journal helps break this self-defeating pattern. Setting aside time for yourself and taking credit for what you do for yourself will help you feel more balanced and more in charge of your own life.

Instructions: Find a journal notebook that is pleasing to you. Look at several styles before you select one. Pick them up, experience the texture and the weight of the journal in your hand. Pick a favorite color or try a pattern or color that is different, wild, soft, something that you wouldn't ordinarily choose. Write in the front of your journal that it belongs to you and you don't want anyone else to read it. Put the next day's date on the first page and write in what you are going to do for yourself tomorrow. If you can't start big, start small. Claiming five minutes of time for yourself is five minutes better than nothing. The next day, after you have given some time to yourself, congratulate yourself in your self-esteem journal for what you did for yourself that day.

How Self-Esteem Develops

Your total self-esteem at any point in your life is a combination of *core self-esteem* (the value you place on yourself at the deepest center of your being), and *situational self-esteem* (the value you place on yourself which is determined by transitory factors such as financial difficulties, illness, undesired weight gain or loss).

Core Self-Esteem

Core self-esteem is in place by age four (McKay and Fanning 2000). It is formed in your earliest relationships and is a result of how your parents or caregivers responded to you. Good core self-esteem is created by loving, nurturing, and supportive adults who are able to recognize and respond to your particular physical and emotional needs. Parents who create good core self-esteem are parents who are able to see you as you really are, not as they hoped you would be.

If you were born into a family where there was serious illness, alcoholism, chaos, or other major stresses, then your beginning may have been compromised in a way that affected your core self-esteem. If your parents were preoccupied with an older sibling who was terminally ill, if they were drinking to excess, using drugs, unable to function adequately in their own lives, then they may have not been able to give you the time, attention, or specific physical and emotional care to nourish your core self-esteem.

If your parents took care of all your physical needs but were emotionally unavailable, then your core self-esteem may have suffered.

The exciting news about core self-esteem is that you can change it. The process is not easy, but you can do it if you are determined to feel better about yourself. In the following chapters, we will provide you with techniques that will help you improve your self-esteem in any area that you think needs work.

It is important for you to understand how your own history affects your total self-esteem so that you are not blaming and self-critical about things that weren't your fault. Even if you have made some bad choices, you need to make the punishment fit the crime. You may have abused substances, been promiscuous, stayed in an abusive relationship. Let yourself think about what you would assign as the appropriate punishment for a girlfriend who had committed these "crimes." Forgiving yourself is so much more difficult than forgiving another. Let yourself be aware that unduly harsh self-blame is toxic to the development of healthy self-esteem.

Finding and refinding the courage to be your own person within the cultural expectations for your gender is a complex and difficult lifelong task. Using the knowledge contained in this book to repair and create a vital and authentic real self, you can move forward into healthy total self-esteem. You can accurately measure and assess your self-esteem assets and deficits component by component. You can learn to make a nonjudgmental inventory of your strengths and weaknesses and set goals for attaining improved skills. You will discover how to monitor your progress and take credit where credit is due. Each time you take credit for a small step toward improved self-esteem, you increase the positive balance in your self-esteem bank account.

Your self-esteem bank account is the amount of available self-esteem you have to draw on at any given point in time. Your self-esteem bank account works just like a regular bank account. When you take positive action in support of yourself or someone else (taking time for yourself, doing something thoughtful for another person, or standing up for yourself when you are scared but when you know you are doing the right thing), you are making a deposit in your self-esteem bank account. When you work past exhaustion day after day, when you neglect your own needs because it is easier for you to take care of others before taking care of yourself, or when you run yourself ragged so as to avoid sadness, anger, loneliness, or feeling excited or sexy, you are making a withdrawal from your self-esteem bank account.

Situational Self-Esteem

Self-esteem is also affected by your situation—the ups and downs of life. You may have impaired self-esteem when you are going through the breakup of a romantic relationship and fabulous self-esteem when you are falling in love. Divorce, illness, the death of a loved one, and financial difficulties can affect self-esteem. It is important to have a framework for understanding how such stresses in life affect your self-esteem so that you can develop positive ways to cope, instead of personalizing the situation so that it affects your total self-esteem.

Situational self-esteem is affected by core self-esteem. If you have good core self-esteem and your boss criticizes something about your work performance, then you probably know how to put this criticism in the context of your overall job performance and not see it as a blow to your value as a person. If you have low core self-esteem, then you may perceive your boss's criticism as the first step on a downward slide to being fired.

Situational self-esteem can also impact core self-esteem. If you missed out on critical learning modules (how to read, how to ride a bike, how to resolve conflicts with peers, how to stand up for yourself, how to conduct yourself in the classroom and on the playground, how to make the transition from girl to young woman), then you may have competency deficits that affect your total self-esteem. Deficits in self-esteem can be caused by frequent geographic moves during childhood, illness or death of a parent, your own illness, poverty, physical disability, and lengthy or traumatic hospitalization.

Self-esteem is an interactive process between you and your world. Positive feedback from the external world (your boss nominates you for an award, your husband sends you flowers unexpectedly) has an impact on your immediate self-esteem, but may not reach to the private core of your deepest self-esteem. You may believe the accolades you receive are based on following the feminine script (being kind, selfless, nurturing, putting others' needs in front of your own) rather than what they are: a positive response to your real worth as a person. If so, your core beliefs about yourself as a woman will not be affected. You will continue to act out the feminine script and feel invisible and undervalued, both by yourself and others.

As a woman, you may neglect your own needs for achievement and fail to acknowledge your feelings, wants, dreams, and desires, even to yourself. This can lead to a situation where you have given too much of yourself away, taking care of others at too great an expense to yourself.

A journey to deeper knowledge of your authentic self will allow you to balance how much you give to others and how much you give to yourself.

Healing Yourself: The Eight Secrets of Self-Esteem

Self-esteem is not an all-or-nothing proposition. We all have it, and we don't. We all have good self-esteem in some areas and underdeveloped self-esteem in others. You may be the top computer salesperson in your company. You may know your computers better than anyone else and be excellent at demonstrating their capabilities. You may be energetic and enthusiastic, and as a result, people tend to buy from you. Your self-esteem in your professional life is strong and healthy.

And yet, you could be paralyzed when it comes to some of your personal relationships. You may have a boyfriend who yells at you and makes you feel terrible. You may have a mother who makes you feel guilty by nagging you about not getting over to see her more often. Your self-esteem in your most intimate relationships is not all you would like it to be.

As you use this book, you will learn how to take credit for your strengths. You will be surprised and excited to discover how much competence you already possess—competence that you already use on behalf of other people. *The Woman's Guide to Total Self-Esteem* will help you learn how to use these skills for your own growth and development.

In each chapter you will find suggestions and exercises to help you work on problems or inadequacies. There may be some chapters that resonate more fully with you than others. For instance, you may have already done a great deal of work with "Getting Off the Emotional Tightrope," so you might read chapter 5 quickly, taking credit for all your hard work and accomplishments in this area. You may find that another component, such as "Accepting Your Body When You Really Hate It" (chapter 3), is giving you some difficulty.

It is important to realize that, as human beings, we are by nature flawed and imperfect. Perfection is an ideal; we may strive toward it, but we will never fully attain it. And that's okay! Face it; you are going to have episodes of overeating or slamming down the phone on your mother. You are human, not a robot, so you are not going to be perfect.

Nobody's Perfect

None of us are perfect. You will never be the perfect mother to your children. Being a good mother means that you do your job adequately most of the time. If you are a good mom, there is a high probability that you are going to raise good kids. You will not be the perfect wife, perfect daughter, perfect employee, or perfect friend. But with some effort and some courage, you can be more than satisfactory at all those things. Sometimes you may fall short of how you would like to handle a particular situation with your boss or your children. At other times, you may be exhilarated by handling a situation superbly.

Tips About How to Use This Book

The 75 Percent Rule: How to set goals that move you quickly toward success. Most of us sabotage our own efforts to improve self-esteem by setting goals and expectations for accomplishment and change that are unrealistically high. We are then unable to meet the goal and thus unknowingly undermine our own self-esteem. It is more self-enhancing to achieve something, no matter how small, than to achieve nothing. The most effective approach in setting goals is to cut the initial expectation by 75 percent and state this as your desired achievement.

For example, if you want to exercise four days a week, recalculate your desired goal and set as your target that, for now, you will exercise one day a week. Anything in addition is gravy and should also be recorded in your self-esteem journal. If you would like to set aside one hour a day for time for yourself, start with setting aside fifteen minutes and record your progress.

Pick one technique. Pick one self-esteem building activity and do it on a regular basis. Conduct your own experiment to see how engaging in even one self-esteem enhancing technique with consistency can have a high payoff for you.

CHAPTER 2

Developing Healthy Selfishness

Healthy selfishness—the very phrase is jarring and foreign. Women are taught to think that it is bad to be selfish. We have been taught to give the bigger piece of the pie to someone else, to let someone else go first, to always be "nice" and defer to others. This chapter will show you how a healthy dose of selfishness is the cornerstone of good self-esteem. If you don't have enough healthy selfishness, the exercises in this chapter will help you learn how to create it.

Healthy selfishness is the belief that you deserve to have your needs met adequately, to express your thoughts and feelings, and to have good things in all areas of your life, recognizing that others deserve the same good things as you.

Most women are crippled in the area of healthy selfishness. We often give away too much of ourselves, reflexively and unconsciously. The feminine script teaches girls and women that our worth comes from our relationships with others. When we concentrate on meeting the needs of others as the primary way to achieve self-esteem, we neglect our own needs. Allowing your sense of self to rest entirely in the hands of others is too risky. You need to be able to identify your own needs and develop a plan to get your needs met.

It is important to distinguish between healthy selfishness and unhealthy selfishness, which can take one of two forms:

1. Impoverished selfishness is the belief that you don't deserve to have your needs met adequately, or to express your thoughts and feelings, or to have good things in all areas of your life.

2. Inflated selfishness is the belief that you deserve to have your needs met perfectly at all times and to express your thoughts and feelings in any way that you want, without regard to the feelings and sensibilities of others. If you have inflated self-ishness, you believe you deserve to have good things in all areas of your life, even if others don't.

Your self-esteem is the result of a complex series of factors inter-acting over time, from your earliest years. "Studies of young children show clearly that parents' style of child-rearing during the first three or four years determines the amount of self-esteem that a child starts with" (McKay and Fanning 2000, 2). During these years good parents help their child create a foundation of healthy selfishness that will be critical to her self-esteem.

Good parenting encourages balance. As infants, we are born thinking that the world revolves around us. In the best of all possible worlds, proper nurturing doesn't knock our sense of self-importance out of us (leading to impoverished selfishness) or encourage inflated selfishness, but rather it establishes a balance of healthy selfishness.

This is not the best of all possible worlds. Even good parents inculcate the feminine script, which actually lowers girls' self-esteem. Parents teach the feminine script to their daughters because it was taught to them. Most parents are not aware of how they promulgate the feminine script; they would be horrified to know that teaching the feminine script encourages their girls to sometimes enslave them-selves to relationships. Good parents teach their daughters to be sen-sitive to the needs of others, to be giving, to be cooperative. There would be nothing wrong with this teaching if it were balanced with encouraging girls to do, to achieve, to conquer their worlds. But most girls are encouraged to find worthiness and competence in how they relate to others.

The masculine script has its own costs; boys are taught not to feel, not to express any feeling but anger, not to be emotionally liter-ate (Kindlon and Thompson 1999). Boys are encouraged to find self-esteem through competence and worthiness that is defined as doing, winning, achieving, problem solving. "Perhaps because men enjoy so much power and prestige in society, there is a tendency to view boys as shoo-ins for future success and to diminish the impor-tance of any problems they might experience in childhood" (p. 6).

Researchers agree that most males tend to focus more on them-selves than others and that females tend to focus on the relationship between themselves and others (Bakan 1966).

Parents need to become more aware of the costs of the feminine and the masculine scripts that they teach. Both boys and girls need to be freer to become who they really are, rather than being limited by the parameters of the masculine and feminine scripts.

Healthy Childhood Development: The First Four Years

Thinking back over your own childhood, consider to what extent your parents encouraged healthy selfishness in you. As you read about how good parents support their child's development, think about the degree to which your own parents nurtured and supported the development of both competence and worthiness in you—and where your parents fell short. Later, in chapter 9, you will have the opportunity to use what you've learned, to help you to become the parent to yourself that you always wanted.

Birth Through One Year

Good parents respond to a particular infant as though she is one of a kind. Although they may be seasoned parents, they know that each infant has her own temperament, her own specific timetable, her own unique personality and process of maturing. They provide safety and consistency in meeting the infant's physical and emotional needs. They are so attuned to their baby that they can tell when she needs soothing and they help the baby calm herself when she is over stimulated or overtired.

They know that even a newborn has ways to calm herself. She can close her eyes, she can go to sleep, she can turn away from stimulation, she can tune out. If she still can't calm herself, they rock her or cuddle her or pat her or sing her to sleep.

If their baby is too withdrawn or lethargic, not able to take enough interest in her world, these parents provide experiences that capture their baby's attention. They invite her to interact with her world. Research has demonstrated that infants are constructing their own complex thinking and feeling and sense experience of their world from the moment of birth (Stern 1985).

Good parents mirror their baby, smiling when she smiles. They use feeling words like "angry, sad, sleepy, scared, happy, excited," to describe what they sense the baby might be feeling. They acknowledge the baby and her needs verbally and non-verbally. It is estimated that at least 90 percent of human communication occurs through nonverbal behaviors (Mehrabian 1972).

This mutual interactive process between parents and child is like a dance. Within the first week of life the baby can distinguish between specific adults through the use of her senses. If the parents and baby dance well together, bonding and deep attachment take place over time. The quality of the bonding rests in large part on how the baby will respond to her increasingly wide world. Parents' ability to support the development of healthy selfishness will determine whether the baby sees the world as a safe place, how much she trusts that others will respond appropriately to her needs, and whether she feels absolutely lovable and valued for just being herself.

As the baby develops better gross and fine motor coordination, she is able to initiate more independent behaviors. Between six and eight months she learns to roll or crawl and moves out more into her world. Parents have to be able to tolerate dependency and support separateness, often quite a juggling act as their baby tries out new behavior, gets scared, and rushes back to the safe home base.

One Year to Two Years

Good parents encourage each of their baby's movements toward mastery. They have to be able to put up with gooshy food smears, pots and pans scattered all over the kitchen floor, the horrible sound of the atonal xylophone or the irritating drums that a friend with no children brought as a gift. They have to avoid being pushy or demanding, so their toddler can explore at her own pace and feel acknowledged for every little increment of mastery. Picasso-like scribbles, mushy Play-doh wads, the act of holding up her arms so Mommy can put on the T-shirt more easily: all these little triumphs have to be applauded, praised, so it seems as if the baby were receiving a Nobel prize many times a day.

Good parents also set limits, so their baby begins to know that the stove is hot, the cat's tail is not for pulling, that she is not to hit or bite or kick other kids or her parents. The baby begins to learn the meaning of the word "no," more clearly. Speech has really taken off in this period and the baby is rewarded verbally and affectionately for approximations of word parts, and then words.

The baby is particularly interested in others of her own kind. Her face lights up and her eyes widen when she sees other babies, toddlers, and children. Her parents encourage her social exploration, setting firm limits as needed for their baby's protection and safety. They may feel a mixture of joy and sadness as their baby passes through the developmental milestones of crawling, walking, and running. They may feel ambivalent as their baby is more and more able to say "no," and back it up with oppositional behavior. She doesn't want to get off the swings, doesn't want to stop digging in the sandbox, doesn't want to go to bed, doesn't want to follow directions. Her parents understand that their baby's strong assertion of her will is appropriate and necessary for her to develop into an assertive and independent person. They move through the frustrating and difficult battle of wills with maturity and humor. Sometimes they don't do it right, but they are good enough at their job.

Two Years to Four Years

The young child is more and more interested in other kids, although she sometimes acts more aggressive or passive than is appropriate. Her parents give her information about what behaviors are okay and not okay, which helps her learn how to interact better with other children. At age two, she has no interest in sharing anything with anyone, other than her dolls. Her parents assist her in understanding the concept of sharing and how it feels when others don't share with her. She gradually learns, difficult step by difficult step, to share with others, at least some of the time.

The child's world continues to enlarge. She is interested in learning how to write her letters. She learns how to ride a bike. She gradually reveals her good sense of humor, sometimes in ways that her parents don't appreciate, as when she imitates some of their less attractive behavior. She has learned how to dress herself, and by three or four, wants to choose her own outfits every morning. Her parents support her choices where possible, but they draw the line at wearing a tutu to preschool on a snowy day.

The child's parents are delighted with her increasing mastery of her world. Her vocabulary is growing by leaps and bounds, and sometimes they have to suppress a laugh when she uses a word or phrase in an unintentionally funny way. She exults in throwing a ball, running, jumping, going to the park to climb the monkey bars. Puzzles and paints, crayons and markers, allow her to be expressive. She often sings tunes she has heard or makes up on her own. Her parents are flexible enough when she is sick or tired. They continue to marvel at the excitement with which she greets the simple events of everyday life. They feel blessed.

Parenting Styles

The three basic parenting styles identified by Baumkind (1968) are the authoritarian, permissive, and the authoritative. Sometimes parents display a mix of these parenting styles. In two-parent families, it is often the case that each parent will have a different style or mixture of styles.

As you read, think about what style of parenting best characterizes your own upbringing.

Authoritarian Parenting

Authoritarian parents tend to be intrusive, demanding (whether overtly or in a subtle fashion), perfectionistic, critical, rigid, and unyielding. Authoritarian parents are unable to respond to the uniqueness of their child. They are unable to engage in a reciprocal relationship with their child, allowing the individuality of their child to influence their parenting. They are unreasonably controlling and convey to their children the belief that the world is a dangerous place. Children of authoritarian parents learn to be distrustful of their environment and the people in it. They are sometimes afraid of new experiences, frightened to get too close to others, apprehensive and fearful, or bully-like and aggressive (to mask their fear) in their involvement in games or activities with other children.

Children raised in authoritarian families tend to be under assertive, and either passive or overly aggressive. They often withhold their inner feelings from parents and others, even from themselves. They often do not know what they feel because they have insulated themselves from the brutal or neglectful behavior of their parents. They learn to numb themselves emotionally, sometimes even physically. Children from authoritarian families are often perceived by others as overly sensitive and inappropriately reactive. They sometimes magnify or minimize physical injuries. They may develop chronic illnesses. These behaviors are often unconscious attempts by the child to cope the best she can and protect herself from being psychologically swallowed up or engulfed by intrusive parenting.

Children from authoritarian families have low self-esteem, whether expressed in passive tentativeness or bossy superiority. As adults, they tend to be rigid in their bodies and to treat their bodies as a thing or machine. They often tend to perceive their parents as all-powerful and themselves as flawed and defective. More rarely, they perceive their parents as flawed and defective and themselves as superior. They are often perfectionists.

Authoritarian parents tend to be intrusive verbally and physically. Their own shaky self-esteem and underdeveloped identity renders them unable to create a balance of initial healthy dependency and trust between themselves and their child. They find it difficult to provide increasing support of independent behavior as the child matures. To authoritarian parents, children are not separate, unique, and individual, but appendages and extensions of the parent.

At best, authoritarian parents support the development of competence in a child. Children from authoritarian families have not been helped to feel worthy, just for being who they are, poopy diapers and all.

Permissive Parenting

Permissive parents allow their child to make her own decisions without providing appropriate guidance and guidelines. Permissive parents may be very loving and tuned in to the feelings of their child, but they find it difficult to set appropriate limits on her behavior.

Permissive parents are wishy-washy about continuity and structure in the home. They often let their child stay up too late, get up too late, eat inappropriately, and make too many decisions about how things will be done in the home. Children of permissive parents learn to use whining, crying, begging, manipulation, and deal-cutting to get their own way.

What permissive parents don't understand is that their child needs structure and limits in order to feel safe and secure. When a permissive parent sets a bedtime and then waffles, the parent may think she is making her child feel special and loved. What the child feels at the deepest level is scared, because when she fights the bedtime rule and the parent gives in, the child psychologically cannot "find" (bump up against) the parent. This leaves the child feeling alone and abandoned. Permissive parents may have been raised in families that were unduly harsh and authoritarian and their permissiveness may be a reaction to their own unfortunate early experience.

Children raised by permissive parents are sometimes bossy and intrusive. They have been running the show at home. When they try the same behaviors with peers, they often experience a rude awakening. Children raised by permissive parents often don't feel really loved.

At best, the child of permissive parents may feel worthy. The child in a permissive family usually has to seek the structure of mastery and competence on her own.

Authoritative Parenting

Authoritative parenting blends appropriate parental limit-setting with warmth and empathy. The authoritative parent sets reasonable limits and guidelines for her child's behavior and does her best to explain the reason for the rule in a way that the child can understand. "You have to go to bed at eight o'clock, so you can get enough sleep to feel good tomorrow. It's not okay to hit the dog; it hurts the dog. You wouldn't like it if someone hit you."

The authoritative parent is empathic. If the child is angry, the authoritative mom or dad will help a two-year-old channel the anger into banging on the play hammer bench and will also encourage her to label her feelings. The child is encouraged to express herself. She can say to her authoritative parent, "I'm mad at you," and not get punished for it.

Authoritative parents are interested in what their child feels and thinks. Wherever possible, they give her a voice in what happens. "Should we have spaghetti or soup for dinner tonight?" Authoritative parents draw the line on decisions that affect the health and welfare of the child. They are willing to incorporate her preferences wherever appropriate. The child of authoritative parents feels respected and that her feelings and opinions really matter. Authoritative parents believe that children should be seen and heard and that the responsibility for structuring decision-making lies with the parent, with lots of input from the child.

Authoritative parents are able to support the development of competence and worthiness in the child.

After the First Four Years

Core self-esteem is in place by age four. Core self-esteem affects how a girl functions throughout the rest of childhood and adolescence. A young girl with good core self-esteem is curious, exuberant, full of spirit, playful, interested. She is able to take pleasure in mastery and learning. As she moves out into a more complicated social world, she comes into contact with teachers and peers. She is also more influenced by the media. She is educated in more detail by peers and teachers about the feminine script. "It's not nice to be angry. Give him the toy. Girls aren't supposed to push. Let her go in front of you."

The self-esteem of girls is affected in childhood and adolescence by the ever expanding array of significant and distant others who pass on the values of the feminine script.

As she reaches the end of elementary school, she has almost always learned to defer to boys in sports and math. In middle school, the power of her peer group is at its most potent. Often in middle school, her grades slip, she loses interest in anything but her friends, and becomes a slave to what others may think of her. She often becomes her own worst enemy: a pimple can seem like the end of the world, exclusion by the popular clique can lead to devastating depression. In middle school for girls, it's all about what's on the outside. Are you a preppie, a jock, a skater, a stoner? Appearance is everything. Many girls lose themselves and their self-esteem in middle school. The media deluges these thirteen- and fourteen-year-old girls with sex, drugs, rap. In middle school, you might be embarrassed to be a virgin.

There is often a little more slack for girls by the time they get to high school if they haven't succumbed to addiction of some kind. Girls who have made it to high school with some self-esteem intact are sometimes able to find an interest group or club or sport or activity that allows them mastery.

It is practically impossible for good parents to protect their daughters from the ravages of the culture which objectifies girls and women and makes it appear that what's on the outside (looks, clothes, a perfect body) is more important than what's on the inside.

In the upcoming chapter, we look in greater detail at how the objectification of women influences our self-esteem.

Exercise: Discovering the Impact of Parenting Style on Your Self-Esteem

The purpose of this exercise is to help you understand more about how the parenting styles of those who raised you has influenced your self-esteem.

1. Make a list of the characteristics of your parents. For example: rigid, demanding, loving, supportive, strict, mean, cruel, accepting, flexible, physically affectionate, fun.

2. Next to each parenting characteristic, rate how frequently your parents engaged in this behavior: seldom, frequently, never.

3. Describe how you felt when your parent behaved in this way and the affect it had on your self-esteem.

Exercise: Experiencing the Fun and Excitement of a Healthy Childhood

The purpose of this exercise is to help you experience more fun, more spontaneity, more excitement, to help you feel more worthy and increase your healthy selfishness.

Try some of the following activities and add to the list. You can add to the list by asking friends and acquaintances what they do for fun. You can also add to the list by observing children at play.

1. Go to the library and get some very bad joke books. Read the jokes out loud to yourself and anyone else who will listen. Tape yourself reading the jokes and crack yourself up when you listen to or watch the tape.

2. Go on an adventure. Break out of your usual pattern. If you usually go to the symphony, go to a rock concert. If you usually eat meat and potatoes, go in search of exotic cuisine. If you never curse, try out some mild swearing. If your language is blue, clean it up. If you usually drink coffee, drink tea. Eat breakfast in the evening and try supper in the morning.

3. Go see a hilarious video or movie.

4. Organize a kid's game with friends: soccer, kickball, tetherball, Monopoly. Play on a jungle gym, a swing, or a slide.

5. Build a sand castle. Take a picture of it. Have the picture enlarged and frame it.

6. Play a game of marbles. Start a collection and play often.

7. Go to a toy store and buy yourself a toy, a game, a doll, or a surprise.

8. Get and use some finger paints or clay.

9. Even if you were told you had no musical talent, go to a music supply store and get bells, a cheap drum or xylophone, flute or triangle. Or make do with what you have at home. Turn on the stereo and become the star you always wanted to be. Use a chopstick for a conductor's baton. Make as much noise as you can allow yourself without annoying the neighbors.

10. Make mud pies.

11. Shoot some hoops.

12. Go to a beauty college and get your nails done.

13. Run along the ocean, lake, or river's edge and make big splashes.

14. Run through the sprinkler.

15. Have a picnic on the living room floor.

16. Buy a garish, sultry, mysterious, cool, or traditional hat on clearance and wear it to work.

17. Buy a whistle and blow it.

18. Play Frisbee.

19. Go to an amusement park or fair and ride the roller coaster, throw darts, or do something that looks like fun and that you would normally never do.

20. Get a jar with a lid, hide it, and start saving for a secret desire that you keep putting off. Secret desires could include: a ride in a hot-air balloon; getting a professional photograph or portrait done; a ride in a glider; taking three months of dance lessons (tap, belly dance, funk, jazz—something you have always secretly wanted to try), voice lessons, or an art class.

Exercise: Giving Treats to Yourself

This exercise will help you give to yourself. These treats are not rewards for good behavior or achievement. This exercise is designed to help you feel more worthy and deserving, just because you exist.

Take three sheets of paper and put the following titles on each page: small treats, medium treats, and large treats. Take a few moments and allow your mind to drift and begin to imagine yourself as deserving a wonderful variety of goodies. Begin small, and then gradually allow yourself to expand your treat horizons. You can keep the lists and add to them as you feel more worthy to receive.

Small treats might include: time to read; time to be with a friend; a delicious breakfast at a restaurant; time to stare off into space and do nothing; a stolen nap; a long luxurious bath followed by a warm oil massage; a makeover at a local department store; taking a complete day off with no errands or tasks for anyone else.

Medium treats might include: a special day or weekend with your spouse, lover, or a dear friend; a trip to a special musical event or coveted restaurant; a massage; four sessions with a trainer to jump-start your exercise program; the purchase of a longed-for item.

Large treats might include: the purchase of a house or condo; going on a special trip or vacation; taking off a month from work.

Give yourself one small treat a week, one medium treat every two weeks, and one large treat whenever you can afford it.

Exercise: Remember Past Successes

The purpose of this exercise is for you to feel more worthy and competent by reviewing situations that you handled well.

You have experienced a number of situations in which you felt good about your performance. Get out some paper and make a list of situations where you would give yourself an A or a B for how well you did. Your list of past successes might include: helping a friend or family member; completing an important part of a project at work; giving a compliment to someone who really needed it; receiving a compliment graciously; having a family member tell you they love you; telling another person you love them; pursuing a task which caused you anxiety; winning a poetry contest; making the soccer team; making the dean's list; learning how to play the flute; writing a short story; making other people laugh.

In order to build your self-esteem, you will have to change some of your ideas about what is worthy of praise; you may withhold rewarding yourself except for extraordinary accomplishments. The fact is, everyday life is made up of ordinary accomplishments. The most likely way to achieve extraordinary things is to reward all achievement, especially the small mundane accomplishments of everyday life.

Exercise: Complete a Task and Take Credit for It

This exercise helps you take conscious credit for completing a task adequately. Completing the task adds an increment to your quotient of feeling competent. Taking credit increases your quotient of feeling worthy.

Write a list of tasks that you feel competent to perform. Perform one of the tasks, take credit for it in your self-esteem journal, and then bask in the good feelings of satisfaction. Such tasks might include: cooking, cleaning, washing the car, writing a letter, paying some bills, exercising. Enjoy the process of doing something you are able to do well, and then congratulate yourself. If you find that you can't in this moment identify anything you do well, go on a walk and take credit for that.

CHAPTER 3

Accepting Your Body When You Really Hate It

To build a sound structure for healthy self-esteem, it is important to accept your own physical structure, your body. Ideally, you want your body to be healthy, fit, and strong. You want to be free from physical illness, living in radiant good health. You want to be attuned to your body, so you know when it needs water, food, or rest. You want your body to be in good shape, so you can enjoy exercise, or sports, and have enough energy to get through even a grueling day at work. What you want is glowing good health and body acceptance.

Body acceptance is being comfortably related to your physical self and having a kind and cooperative relationship with your body. The woman who is comfortably related to her body can listen to her body. She knows when she feels healthy, fit, and strong. She hears her body's signals. The woman who is deeply connected to her body knows that having a strong body makes it easier to deal with crises and emotional trauma. She also is sensitive to changes in her body, so that a slight increase in lower back muscle tension may cue her to do some slow stretching and avoid a back problem.

Body rejection is being uncomfortable with your physical self and having an adversarial or neglectful relationship with your body. The woman who is uncomfortably related to her body has difficulty listening to her body's wants and needs. She may not exercise appropriately; she may compulsively exercise when she shouldn't. She is unable to figure out what her body is telling her about what she should eat, when she should rest, and when she needs medical attention.

The Illusion That Perfection Is Possible

Body acceptance is one of the areas in which we women routinely sabotage our own self-esteem—not because we want to, but because we don't know what to do to have a more cooperative relationship with our own bodies. As women, we are not taught to be proud and respectful of our bodies. There is tremendous cultural pressure to have a "perfect" body. Billboards and magazines plaster photographs everywhere of ultra-slim, ultra-beautiful women, and these "advertised" women have been absorbed into our awareness as the icons we often try to imitate.

They become our false goddesses. We see men and women looking at the photographs and admiring them, and we want to be admired too. So we try to match the unattainable standard and criticize ourselves for being unable to achieve the impossible. The Eating Disorders Awareness and Prevention Center reports that in the year 2000, the average American woman is five-foot-four and weighs 140 pounds. The average American model is five-foot-eleven and weighs 117 pounds. The average fashion model is thinner than 98 percent of American women.

The center also reports that 42 percent of first-through-third grade girls want to be thinner and that 81 percent of ten-year-old children are afraid of being fat. The center states that half of nine- and ten-year-old girls feel better about themselves if they are on a diet and that almost half of these little girls are dieting some of the time. The center finds that almost half of American women are on a diet on any given day and that 25 percent of American males are on a diet on a given day.

These statistics are shocking. Meanwhile, the incidence of obesity in children and adults has increased rapidly in the last thirty years, with the most dramatic increases occurring in the last decade. "Though eating disorders are found in every culture, they are much more common in the most industrialized, technologically advanced, countries where individualistic achievement is stressed" (Hartley 1998).

Girls and women are caught in an excruciating dilemma: increasing pressure to conform to the idealized media images versus the reality that girls and women are gaining more weight by the day. Overweight and obese children and adults are frequently the target of derision, scorn, and contempt. This vicious treatment contributes to lowered self-esteem and sometimes increases the probability that those with weight problems will try to comfort themselves with food.

This reality sets women up for failure. Most of us are never going to look like models or women in the media. Never, no matter what we do to ourselves. Even models can't look like their photographs without special lighting, makeup, and airbrushing. Most women (95 percent of all women) are unable to attain the ideal cultural body type. We are not genetically programmed for that kind of body.

We sometimes starve ourselves to try to attain the cultural ideal. Women have elected a variety of interventions to try to have the perfect body: liposuction, laser surgery, dermabrasion. Sometimes these procedures produce the desired results and other times they backfire. Many of our clients who have had their breasts enhanced, either because they were insecure about their looks or because their boyfriends or husbands asked them to do it, have told us that their breasts don't feel natural. One client said that the implants had hardened into stone. While she once was proud of showing off her big breasts, now, ten years later, she has become extremely uncomfortable.

The Objectification of Women

Fredrickson and Roberts (1997) introduced the concept of objectification to describe how American culture acts as though we women were only our bodies, to the exclusion of all other dimensions of identity. The most damaging result of the objectification of women is that many women self-objectify: we become preoccupied with our own physical appearance, excluding other aspects of selfhood such as intelligence, compassion, and competence.

When we self-objectify, we focus on our physical attractiveness, coloring, weight, sex appeal, measurements, and muscle tone. When we do not self-objectify, we focus instead on our muscular strength, physical coordination, stamina, health, physical fitness, and physical energy level.

Self-objectification can have dangerous consequences for women. Noll and Fredrickson (1998) found that self-objectification increases body shame, which is in turn linked to an increased risk for disordered eating.

The Damage to Self-Esteem Caused by Distorted Body Image

Instead of accepting our bodies as they are, many of us begin to hate our bodies for not measuring up to unrealistic cultural ideals. Most of us have done this unconsciously since childhood or adolescence. Once a woman has absorbed a negative body image of herself, it is hard for her to have any kind of complete positive self-esteem. All she can think is, "I'm not good enough. I'm not thin enough. I'm fat. I'm ugly." Or, less frequently, but no less painfully, "I'm thin as a skeleton and I've never been able to gain weight, no matter what I eat."

All the research shows that most of us, regardless of our appearance, are unhappy with our bodies. Most women have a negatively distorted body image: what we believe about how our bodies look is not congruent with how other people perceive us. We see ourselves as grossly fat while others see us as attractive. In fact, many women who do have the culturally perfect body believe that their bodies are flawed. It is their perception of their bodies that is flawed and which produces a distorted body image.

A distorted body image creates negative self-esteem. A deep dissatisfaction with your body will hasten a descent into anxiety and depression, a downward spiral of self-loathing and self-devaluation.

Your Automatic Debit Account: How You Transfer Negative Feelings Onto Your Body

Many of us unconsciously transfer internal feelings of deficiency or inadequacy onto our bodies. Our body becomes the representation of a whole emotional experience. Imagine a woman getting ready to accompany her husband to his office Christmas party. She completes her makeup, gets dressed, comes out into the living room, and says to her husband, "Do I look fat in this?" If we could see inside her psyche, we would know that she is feeling nervous and apprehensive about the party. She, unfortunately, has transferred her anxious feelings into concern about how she looks, and she is not even aware that she did it. If she had been aware of her feelings, she could have talked to her husband about her nervousness and asked for his reassurance.

Unconsciously, she has translated emotional feelings into a concern about her body and how others perceive her. Culture has trained her to do this. Cultural training has made her believe that how she looks on the outside represents who she is as a person.

The translation of emotional concerns into anxiety about our bodies is a process set in motion by learning the feminine script in childhood and adolescence. We learn to objectify ourselves, to judge ourselves by the current cultural standard. If culture dictates that the most important thing about being a woman is how we look, then it is difficult not to assume that bad feelings are somehow related to our bodies and how we appear. For example, a girl or woman may have the feeling, "I'm unhappy. I'm miserable. I'm worthless." But she unconsciously and automatically changes those painful feelings into, "I'm fat. My thighs are heavy. I'm ugly." "Fat" or "ugly" becomes the mantra of her sense of self and overwhelms all other potential sources of self-definition and well-being. Not knowing how to cope with "bad" or unpleasant feelings, she believes, "If only I can change something about my body, I'll feel better."

In this way, the pain of self-hatred becomes highly focused and directed. Instead of nebulous and free-floating feelings of anxiety and unworthiness, a woman feels she knows exactly what is wrong with her: her body is wrong. Her hips are too large, her stomach is too fat. Her breasts are too large or too small or the wrong shape. Her thighs are huge or dimpled with cellulite. If she had a better body, she thinks, she would have a better life.

A woman can take comfort in thinking like this. Instead of figuring out why she is unhappy, and taking steps to change her life on a deeper level, she has transferred her feelings to a more superficial level, onto her body. This is not her fault, she has been trained by cultural expectations to equate her worth as a person with how she looks. From this pattern of thinking, she obtains a sense of control. She will change her body, perhaps by any means she can.

Most women need a lot of help with body acceptance. Many of us are absolutely unable to perceive our bodies as they really are. Our image of ourselves is warped and out of line with the reality of how we appear. If this applies to you, as it does to most women, you need to start now to build a better relationship with your body. You don't have to like your body. It may seem to you that it is flawed. You may not like the blemishes on your skin, or old scars, and you may think you are too fat. You need to begin to understand that most of your dislike of your body has been created by the women's training program that values form over substance.

Although we may hate our physical bodies, and try to starve them and run them to exhaustion and disregard their needs for food and water and rest, our bodies are the temples in which we live. It is within our own special, unique body that we exist on earth.

Acknowledging Your Body

Your body is your great friend, and you need to accept it as such. This is difficult for most women. It may be helpful to look at the different factors that go into creating healthy body acceptance or unhealthy body rejection.

Body Type and Body Image

Your body type is primarily determined by your genetic inheritance. Gabriel Cousens, M.D. (1986) has summarized the information on body type characteristics using ideas from Chinese medicine and Ayurvedic medicine from India, both based on philosophies thousands of years old. Chinese medicine studies the health of the human body through the lens of five elements: earth, air, water, fire, and ether (space). Ayurveda is simpler, reducing the five elements into three primary body types: *kapha* (earth/water); *pitta* (fire); and *vata* (ether/air). Characteristics of each body type and combinations of body types have served as reliable indicators for diagnosis and treatment of health problems.

Cousens notes that most of us are some blend of the characteristics of all three body types, usually with one body type predominating. He describes the kapha body type as heavy, having smooth thick skin and thick lustrous hair, large eyes, mouth, and teeth, and having stable appetites. The kapha body type prefers not to be very active and is cool, calm, and complacent. The pitta body type has a medium-balanced build, fine straight hair, fiery eyes, and brisk appetites, with good endurance unless overheated. The pitta's emotional style is angry, forceful, incisive, and impatient.

The vata body type is tall and rangy with lean dry hair and skin, small eyes, irregular teeth, and a variable appetite. Vata types have poor stamina and are light sleepers. Their emotional climate is fearful and anxious, spacey and changeable.

You've inherited your body type from your ancestors. You may have wide hips, narrow shoulders, long graceful fingers, gorgeous thick hair, and muscular legs. You can't change your body type, but you can learn to acknowledge its reality. You can set reasonable goals of increasing your strength, endurance, and flexibility so that you can begin to have some experience of feeling good in your body.

Body Type: Jeanne's Story

Like many women, Jeanne spent years trying every new diet, every new exercise, reading every new book on weight loss. No matter how hard she tried, she just couldn't change the shape of her body.

One day, while visiting her mother, Jeanne looked at some old family photographs. She was shocked. What she saw in the pictures were her mother, who had died when Jeanne was ten, and her mother's mother, and her mother's mother's mother. All of these women had the same body type, the same body that Jeanne had been trying so desperately to change! She saw that she came from a long line of Scandinavian peasants, women who worked the land in Sweden. Their lives were very hard. Their days were filled with intense physical labor. Their winters were spent chopping logs and sewing clothing to keep their families warm. In warmer weather they worked the fields, hoeing crops, picking vegetables, and carrying heavy baskets on their backs. Most women bore numerous children, and did the job of mothering along with their other work.

Jeanne realized that she had inherited her particular body type, and that there was a reason for her kind of body to exist. In a land where only the fittest survived, women with her body type outworked and outlived thinner, smaller women. Now, Jeanne and her family have been transplanted to Los Angeles, and she does not do hard physical labor as her ancestors once did. Jeanne realized that she couldn't change her ancestors. She couldn't change who she is. She saw that her life would certainly be happier if she could acknowledge this and accept the strengths of her heritage. She, too, is a hearty woman.

Jeanne's story is repeated in almost every woman's life. You have the body you have because you inherited it. You don't have to like it, but you do have to acknowledge it. Your body is the only one you are ever going to have. Attempts to drastically alter your body usually make you feel worse. You can't help the body you were given at birth.

You *can* choose how you feel about the body you have now. You are in charge of how you care for your body. You can accept and nurture it.

Exercise: Looking at Childhood Photos

The purpose of this exercise is to expand and clarify your memories of yourself growing up. If you are usually harsh and self-critical about how you look, this is an opportunity to see your past with fresh eyes.

Instructions: Go back and find some childhood photos. Take a good look at yourself. Women with body image problems are almost always surprised to discover what they looked like as children. There is always something that they weren't aware of, something unexpected. When available, home movies breathe life into memories, illuminating the faded and lost images of your childhood self. Make two columns and find out the truth. Jeanne's list might look like this:

How I Thought I Looked	How I Actually Looked
Fat and dumpy	Healthy and strong, not fat
Too big, not petite, gross	Big-boned, capable
Homely, ugly	Attractive
Unhappy, depressed	Happy, content

Body Talk and Feelings About Your Body: The Internal Critic

The *internal critic* is the *saboteur* inside you—the ugly thoughts and feelings in your mind that undermine your efforts to improve your self-esteem. The internal critic is a significant determinant of your bad feelings about your body. The dislike many of us feel toward our bodies comes out in angry, accusing thoughts and feelings directed toward ourselves and our bodies.

Most of us would never talk to another person, or even an animal, the way we speak to ourselves. In the privacy of our own minds, we may say vicious, demeaning, cruel things to ourselves much of the time. Or, the attacks from the inside may be more subtle. "I guess I look okay for my age, although I'm disgusted by my cellulite."

Sometimes we're not even consciously aware of the derogatory things we say about ourselves. "I'm a fat pig, I'm ugly, no one will ever be able to love me." These self-destructive thoughts, as well as feelings of self-loathing and contempt, often mutate into negative white noise that perniciously poisons our core self-esteem. Even when our attacks on ourselves are more mild ("I'm never going to lose the last ten pounds. I feel frustrated, helpless, angry, and guilty"), we drain away our precious self-esteem by believing that how we look is the measure of our value and worth.

Most women would never say such things to a friend. Why, then, do we say these terrible things to ourselves? Because we have taken in the cultural ideals of how we're supposed to look. We sit in hostile judgment of our own imperfect bodies. This process devastates our sense of self.

We must begin to recognize what we're doing, and stop. These internal tirades are bad for us, they make us feel guilty, unworthy, and ashamed. When we annihilate our bodies, very little self-esteem is left.

How the Internal Critic Developed

The internal critic is often created by internalized cultural prescriptions of how your body should be. The internal critic can also contain fragments of toxic experience absorbed from important caregivers in your early life. You may have been the object of intense feelings such as anger, frustration, helplessness, or depression belonging to caregivers trying to do their best, sometimes not doing their best, in a difficult situation.

Parents who are having difficulties, such as serious financial difficulties or chronic illness, may have unknowingly leaked toxic feelings into your emotional landscape. War, famine, and civil unrest can also inject the infant or child with feelings of terror, confusion, and "badness."

It is critical on this journey to improved self-esteem to understand that events beyond your control may have significantly shaped some aspects of your core self-esteem. You can't help what happened in your history. You *can* take charge of claiming your self-esteem strengths and repairing your self-esteem weaknesses now.

The Bad News and the Good News

The bad news is that most of us torture ourselves internally with negative thoughts and feelings about our "flawed" bodies. The good news is that what has been taken in from culture to create the *internal critic* can be gradually softened and eventually exorcised. The internal critic is adopted, not born in you; fat babies are not beating themselves up. You learn to hate your body. What you have learned can be changed by you.

Silencing The Internal Critic: Jeanne's Story

Negative self-talk is driven by powerful toxic feelings. Jeanne's internal dialogue probably looked like this:

Negative Self-Talk	Driven by Jeanne's Toxic Feelings
"I hate these flabby thighs."	Self-hatred, disappointment
"I am a fat pig."	Self-loathing, contempt, disgust
"No one will ever love me, because my body is so gross."	Self-hatred, fear
"I will never be able to have a perfect body, so I may as well give up and pig out. Who cares."	Depression, hopelessness, helplessness, resignation victorious. ("After all, my body is the enemy—I just won")

Jeanne needs to learn how to identify the specific unpleasant feelings she is experiencing so that she can stop herself from automatically projecting the bad feelings onto her body. When she is able to identify her feelings and decrease their intensity, Jeanne's self-esteem will grow by leaps and bounds.

Maryanne, Jeanne's best friend, is able to respond more objectively and lovingly to Jeanne's damaging internal dialogue. Maryanne is able to say to Jeanne, when Jeanne is ripping herself to shreds:

Positive Other-Talk	Driven by Objectivity and Loving Feelings
"Get a grip. Some people are starving and you're worried about your thighs. What are you really feeling?"	Concern, tough-love
"Calling yourself names is disrespectful. You don't do that to anyone else. Name one of your good qualities and take credit for it."	Compassion, genuine love, dismay, outrage
"People do love you when you allow yourself to be lovable and loved."	Frustration, anger, love
"It's true, you'll never have a perfect body. No one does. What can you do for five minutes to get in shape?"	Discouraged, frustrated, compassionate, loving

Exercise: Silence Your Internal Critic

The purpose of this exercise is to silence the internal critic in you, to teach you how to respond to negative self-talk.

If your best friend isn't available, become your own best friend. Use the toxic feelings to power the response you'd make to another woman saying destructive things about herself. Make a list of negative thoughts and a second list of responses. You already have the skills to shut up the internal critic; you'd use them in a heartbeat to help someone else.

Exercise: Fight Fire With Fire

The purpose of this exercise is to help use your own anger and frustration to set limits and boundaries on your internal critic.

Develop your own Internal CEO and *fight fire with fire*. Unmask the toxic feelings that power the self-denigrating thoughts and use the feelings to do battle—just as you would for anyone unfairly attacked.

The next time you hear that internal voice, tell it, "Stop! I don't have to listen to that." Say, "Stop!" and when it starts again, use a louder voice and tell it again to stop. The next time you feel loathing toward your body, tell the feeling to get lost, you don't deserve to be treated like that. You can tell the internal critic to "stop" out loud or in the privacy of your own mind.

After you have told your internal critic to stop, you need to say compassionate things to yourself. Say, "You don't deserve to be talked to like that. You are a good person. You are doing the best you can." Whenever the internal critic comes back, tell it, "Shut up. You are just an echo of bad voices I have heard in my life. I'm not going to take it anymore."

Exercise: How to Stop Bad Thoughts and Feelings

The purpose of this exercise is to give you significant relief from unwanted, upsetting, anxiety-provoking thoughts and feelings. This exercise helps you create a powerful container to hold and detoxify horrible thoughts and feelings.

1. Set aside a specific time of day in which to do this exercise. The time allotted should be between twenty-five and thirty minutes. Use a kitchen timer for this exercise so you won't be distracted by watching the time. Use the entire time, even if you have to go over and over the same repugnant thoughts and feelings.

2. You need to schedule this time as seriously as you would schedule a doctor's appointment. Write the appointments for the week in your day planner.

3. In your scheduled time, write down all the ugly scary thoughts and feelings that have been bothering you. Write about financial worries, job problems, and relationship difficulties. Write about anger, sadness, confusion, fear, anxiety, helplessness, and depression. Spew out the disgusting thoughts and feelings. This is not great literature. You don't need to use complete sentences or worry about spelling.

4. When you are finished writing, don't reread what you have written. It would only reinfect you.

5. Rip up or burn what you have written.

6. During the rest of the day, if the awful thoughts and feelings come back, say to yourself, "I don't have to think about this now. I have time set aside to work on this at 5:30."

This exercise is almost miraculous. It will provide you with significant relief in two to three days. If it does not, you need to increase the amount of time you spend writing.

Nutrition

You may be well aware of the kind of nutrition your body needs to be healthy. You may know you need to eat a wide selection of starch, carbohydrates, and proteins, and that you need to have roughage in your daily intake and an adequate amount of water. You may know that foods that are unprocessed are better for you. You may have a good-enough connection with your body to know what to eat to be your most vital, fit, healthy, and vibrant self.

If you do know how to nourish yourself in a healthy way, you are part of a blessed minority. The rest of us are cursed by only thinking we know what our bodies want and need. For most of us, our bodies are telling us honest lies about our nutritional needs.

The Problem

There is so much emphasis for women on what's on the outside (physical attractiveness, coloring, sex appeal, muscle tone, weight, measurements) that we often don't even think to focus on what's on the inside (our muscular strength, physical coordination, stamina, health, physical fitness, energy level). What's on the inside is directly related to what we eat and how we exercise.

Americans spend $33 billion a year on weight loss, with obviously poor results. This focus on the symptom (weight and appearance) obscures the reality that most women don't know how to eat to be healthy and fit. Women have not been helped to know the basics about good nutrition; we have not been taught to listen to our needs for proper nutrition.

The National Institute of Diabetes and Digestive and Kidney Diseases (2000) has compiled some disturbing facts about the problems of obesity and eating disorders in adults and children. They report that 280,000 deaths per year in America are attributed to obesity. More than one-half of the adult U.S. population is overweight.

Twenty-five percent of adult women and almost 20 percent of men are clinically obese. Clinical obesity, anorexia, and bulimia are increasing dramatically in children, adolescents, and adults. Recent research has demonstrated that self-esteem in children declines rapidly as they gain more weight (Strauss 2000).

Diet-related diseases include diabetes, cancer, osteoporosis, and cardiac disease. Many of these diseases are life threatening. Eating disorders, overweight, and obesity constitute a devastating threat to the physical and mental health of children and adults in the industrialized countries of the world.

Health and disease are mediated by genetics and environment. However, there is increasingly alarming evidence that correlates certain kinds of diets (those high in fat, prepackaged denatured foods, most fast food) with startlingly increased risk for illness (Cousens 1986). America leads the world in consumption of erzatz foods, followed by Japan and England (Hartley 1998).

In all industrialized nations in the world, where farming has gone from locally grown foods to processed, denatured convenience foods, people have become confused about what to eat to maintain and create good health. Most of us are so confused about healthy eating that we can't trust our bodies to tell us the truth.

Eating Disorders

Conservative estimates indicate that after puberty, 5–10 percent of girls and women suffer from eating disorders, including anorexia, bulimia, binge eating disorder, or borderline conditions (Eating Disorders and Awareness Prevention Center, 2000). Eating disorders are painful to experience, damaging to your health, and can be life threatening.

If you are ten percent above or below your appropriate weight, if you binge or purge, if you starve and stuff, you may have an eating disorder. Eating disorders need to be taken seriously. If you suspect that you may have an eating disorder, you need to consult an expert: a psychiatrist, psychologist, or physician who specializes in diagnosis and treatment of eating disorders.

The Importance of Good Nutrition

Good nutrition is important for all women. We need to learn how to nourish the woman inside with healthful foods that support our best functioning. Most of us are paying a high price for not understanding the relationship between good nutrition, physical and emotional well-being, and good self-esteem. As women, we need to resist the cultural impetus that defines us by how we appear on the outside. We need to insist that we are worthy of feeling good on the inside.

Most of us don't eat what's good for us. Over the years, we have become confused about what we need to eat to be our most vital selves. We need to go through a retraining program.

The Candy Bar

Your body may produce a craving for a candy bar. A craving, however, is often a false message about what your body really needs to stay healthy and fit. Your body's craving for a candy bar could be:

1. Simply a desire for a sweet taste.

2. A desire for quickly metabolized energy.

3. A quick "fix" to give you immediate gratification when you feel sad, lonely, empty, depressed, anxious. You may be using a physiologic "fix" to take care of an emotional feeling.

4. An automatic habit.

5. A physiologic craving related to your hormonal system.

6. The result of someone rewarding you with sweets as a child.

Chronically meeting your emotional needs with food has negative results. You may have, over time, learned to bypass your real feeling states (sadness, emptiness, self-loathing, excitement) in a way that has become automatic, so the painful scary feelings are never experienced directly. This leaves you without the accurate information you need to deal with your emotional needs directly.

If you are feeling depressed or anxious, and you self-medicate with food, you will find that your path toward healthy self-esteem is blocked. If you are overweight, you may eat a candy bar or a highly processed food and your brain may assess that you need to continue eating because you haven't given your body any "real" (unprocessed) food.

Nutrition Solution: Eating Mindfully

Eating consciously within your best nutritional parameters can be a joyful experience. Use the following guidelines to nourish yourself well.

1. Eat foods as close to nature, organic and unprocessed, as possible.

2. Avoid high-fat, high-sugar foods.

3. If you have difficulty finding organic foods, look for foods with no discernible pesticides.

4. Keep your dairy intake minimal, or stop dairy.

5. Let yourself experience the six basic tastes (bitter, sweet, salty, astringent, sour, pungent) slowly and allow yourself to be completely in the experience of savoring the tastes. The six tastes trigger metabolic processes which help you move toward increased health and balance.

6. Avoid eating in front of the television, at the movies, while reading, or when bored.

7. Put a flower on the table, use a pretty place mat, and tell yourself that you are worth as much care as a guest in your home.

Deepak Chopra (1993) and David Simon (1999) give additional information on healthy eating. Consultation with an experienced nutritional practitioner can individualize your approach.

Exercise: Nutrition Journal

We often have habits that we are unaware of, like buying chocolate bars every time we go to the drugstore or eating cookies whenever we sit down in front of the TV.

The first step toward better eating is to increase your awareness by keeping a food journal. Make yourself aware of what foods you are consuming and why. Tell yourself the truth. If you're willing to tell yourself the truth, you've solved more than half of the problem.

Get out your self-esteem journal and start keeping a record of everything you eat and drink. Be sure to record the amount of everything you eat and drink and the time of day.

Look for patterns in a nonjudgmental way. Say to yourself, "Let's just get the information." It's not in your best interest to stay in denial about what you are eating. You can't change unless you acknowledge where you are. Keep your food journal for a month. Then choose one small change you want to make. Set small achievable goals. Very small. The road to better self-esteem is a road taken, small step by small step.

Just change one thing about your eating pattern. When you do, write it down in your self-esteem journal and take credit for it. Throw away the charts of ideal body weights. Throw away your scales. Even if you and another woman are the same height, you could be very different in your bone mass, structure, and musculature, and thus very different in your right weight. Remember, muscle weighs more than fat. Your goal in nutrition is learning to eat from the inside out. If a woman is really connected to her own guts, she won't starve herself and she won't stuff, because it's uncomfortable. Stuffing and starving are adaptations in which a woman ignores her body. Measure your success by how you feel: strong, fit, radiant, vital, and alive.

How to Take the "Die" Out of Diet

Dieting is a terrible idea, especially when you have decided to work on your self-esteem. Even the word "diet" sounds ominous. The first three letters of the word tell you everything you need to know about the deprivation contained in this negative experience. Diets inevitably lead to overeating, creating additional shame and guilt, which further erodes your self-esteem.

Dieting does not work, not even over the short term. Research on dieting shows that you eventually gain back the weight that you lose on a diet, plus an average of three to five pounds more than when you started (Schwartz 1996). So dieting just means setting yourself up for failure, and that's one thing you don't want to do.

Beware of destructive dieting cycles. You may have tried losing weight by cutting down on eating so that your food intake was only five hundred calories a day. You lost weight, but what you lost was primarily muscle mass. The weight came back, so you cut back to five hundred calories again. And you found that you couldn't lose as much weight as you could the first time you tried.

What happened was your body adapted by decreasing its metabolic rate and changing its "set point." (Schwartz 1996). This means you started gaining weight at lower amounts of caloric input than before you started dieting. Your body's physiology channeled the first calories back into fat cells.

When you deprive your body of calories, your body learns to live on less. Your body is an extremely efficient survival machine. It doesn't listen to your desire to be as skinny as Kate. When you cut back on calories, your body sends out signals to every cell, "There are not many calories available today. Use as few calories as you can because we haven't got any extra stored up."

Dieting is bad for you because it makes you feel deprived. Whenever you are being deprived of something, you will find yourself thinking about it and longing for it. You may be one of many women on diets who easily flips to the other side of deprivation and goes into the "excess" mode. Stuffing and bingeing may be the response.

The way to change your body's set point is through exercise and eating reasonably. Eat in a nutritious way and increase your exercise. If you change your relationship with food to one where you give your body what it needs, not what you have been taught to want, you can, over time, develop a healthy body, a healthy activity level, and good self-esteem.

Physical Exercise

Many women who have problems with body acceptance report that they do no exercise at all. It usually turns out that they have not yet found any exercise they like.

When you are working on your self-esteem, it is helpful to set easily attainable goals and record your progress in your self-esteem journal. Make your progress easy to track. Writing it down records your progress in a special, enduring way. It reinforces what you are doing for yourself. Every time you look at your progress, you experience a sense of accomplishment, creating a chain of events leading to more positive forward movement.

Use Your Skills for Yourself

Take credit for just one thing at a time. This is neither a race nor a competition, and there is no right or wrong way to go about it. It's a matter of keeping careful track of what you're doing for yourself. You probably have wonderful skills for keeping track of other people's needs and accomplishments. If your girlfriend needed to go to the gym three times a week for a health problem, you would support her in any way that you could, or if your daughter wanted to play soccer, you would stretch as much as you could so she could have that experience.

Use these already developed skills for yourself.

When your body feels tuned up, you feel better. You don't tire as easily. Exercise provides great relief from stress, tension, and depression. When you exercise, you are in a better mood. Let the endorphins rip.

Why Exercise Doesn't Come Naturally to Many Women

Exercise is something that males are encouraged to do early on in life. Little boys are applauded for making the football team or soccer team or baseball team. Mothers send their boys out with a basketball to play pickup games in the driveway or on the playground before dinner. Boys are encouraged to ride their bikes to see friends who live several blocks away. Girls have the exact same biological needs for movement and activity, yet girls are seen as more vulnerable and so experience greater restrictions. Girls are often not encouraged, the way that boys are encouraged, to exercise, so girls often don't develop the habit of exercise the way boys do (Pipher 1994). Later in life, it's easier for a woman to stop exercising altogether and, as a result, put on more weight.

Exercise: Physical Exercise

Commit to five minutes a day of any kind of exercise—walk, stretch, move around to music with a compelling beat. Remember, five minutes of *anything* counts. Walking, stretching, dancing. Turning on the radio and swaying to the beat. Anything! Then get out your self-esteem journal and give yourself credit for what you have done. Congratulations! This is your new beginning

Exercise: The Next Step

Break your old patterns. Find some kind of movement you enjoy, and do it regularly. A walk in the woods, a swim in a pool, a night of all-out disco dancing, and your body will feel more fit and you will feel better overall as a result. Consider belly dancing, where real bellies are an asset, or beginning yoga—anything that sounds interesting or calls out to your sense of the exotic. Make sure that the exercise you choose is compatible with your specific physical abilities and health limitations.

The Darker Side: Addicted to Exercise

Several years ago, high impact aerobics were very popular, and millions of women were jumping and skipping and bouncing and pounding and crunching and banging as a regular form of exercise. Many suffered shinsplints, cartilage breakdown, muscle sprains, knee injuries, and lots of wear and tear on their joints, but wouldn't dream of giving it up because it was the thing to do. Some aerobics instructors used to assert, "No pain, no gain." So women unknowingly exercised their bodies into agony. Some people still believe in the "no pain, no gain" idea. But a woman who exercises so intensely is ignoring how her body actually feels.

One woman revealed that she was running twelve miles a day, even though her knee was injured and her doctor had advised against it. "What am I going to do?" she sobbed. She intuitively knew her running had become her way of avoiding her problems.

Just as the woman who does not exercise at all is out of touch with her body in some important way, the woman who exercises her body too much is also out of touch.

One of the most helpful things about physical exercise is that you have to be fully present in the moment to do it safely. It's an enormous relief to be totally immersed in something that makes you feel good and alive.

A woman who is in touch with her body doesn't exercise when she's sick and doesn't exercise on an injury. She enjoys exercise that is appropriate for her health, age, and level of fitness. When you are attuned to your body, it will tell you how much and what kind of exercise you need. Your goal is to feel healthy, fit, and strong. It's empowering to feel strong. Increasing your feeling of connection with your body and your sense of physical strength gives you a better basis on which to continue to build your healthy self-esteem

Body Feedback

You arrive in this world in a unique body. It is important to listen to your body and to respect what you hear. Do you need more exercise?

Are you chronically overtired? Do you respect such basic signals as fear, hunger, fatigue, and depletion?

The truth is, there is only one you, and nobody can do a better job of taking care of yourself than you.

We can all think of examples in ourselves and others which illustrate the high price we pay for ignoring our bodies. Ulcers, arthritis, diabetes, some cardiac disease, cancer, and high or low blood pressure are some of the illnesses that can be brought on by or exacerbated by stress. Weight problems, compulsive exercise or none at all, and treating your body like a "thing" (not resting when you are tired; going hungry when you are famished; exercising on injuries; eating to take care of emotional needs) are indications that you are not fully in your body, and are unable to pay attention to your basic physiologic needs for sustenance, exercise, and rest.

Your body is not a machine but a miraculous collection of individual cells with unique intelligence. Every cell in your body has the information it needs to be completely healthy. You need to begin to retrain yourself so that you can more accurately read and interpret the messages your body sends you about your health and well-being.

The woman who is connected to her body knows immediately when something is wrong. She hears her body's signals. We need to be connected to our bodies from the inside, so we know which of the things that our world offers is right for us.

Feedback: Stacey's Story

Stacey, lively and intelligent, got so caught up in trying to assure herself of an exciting future that she almost wrecked her body. Stacey worked for a big international firm that promised her an executive position in London if she would first work for three years in Alaska. The London position was Stacey's dream job. She'd joined the firm with the idea of one day getting assigned there. So she decided to do as the firm asked and put in the three years in Alaska.

Stacey had always been healthy, but just four weeks after moving to Fairbanks she was besieged by constant illness. She got a cold, then flu, and then allergies. A few months later, she got the first migraine headache she'd ever had. Then she was hit by a terrible depression. Stacey's therapist asked her how she felt about living in Alaska.

"I can't stand it here," she snuffled. "It's like a foreign planet. I can't stand the snow and the creepy darkness. I feel like a fish out of water."

A "fish out of water" can't survive. But Stacey wouldn't ask for a transfer. She was afraid to make waves. She didn't want to speak up about her unhappiness and run the risk of upsetting her boss. She was trying to follow the feminine script at too great cost to herself.

Other people in the firm who loved Alaska surrounded Stacey. They appreciated the wildness and the frontier feeling. They were glad to leave big cities and pollution problems behind. Alaska was great for a lot of people, but not for Stacey. Her body was trying to signal her on an immediate, physical level. It was trying to tell her in every way it could that she needed to move. She needed sun and warmth and her familiar family and friends. Stacey wouldn't listen.

Finally, Stacey developed a painful case of irritable bowel syndrome. She became so ill that she had to take a medical leave from her job. While recovering at her mother's home in California, she realized that she could not face going back. She sent the company notice that she had quit.

Stacey was so strong in her desire to be successful that she ignored the signals from her body that something was wrong. Eventually her mistake caught up with her.

Exercise: Learning to Listen to Your Body

The purpose of this exercise is to help you develop a closer communicative relationship with your body. This will allow you to get more accurate information from your body about health, emotions, wants, desires, and needs.

Start at the tips of your toes and slowly move your attention into your feet. Focus there.

See exactly what sensations and feelings you can be aware of in your ankles and feet. Move systematically up your body, slowly, noticing feelings, sensations of warmth, coolness, tingling, anything at all. You may be amazed at how much information your body will provide for you if you take the time to tune in. See what your body is telling you.

Try this exercise in the morning when you first wake up. Do the exercise midday at work. Check in with your body after work, after exercise, after having some fun, after sex or cuddling, after a wonderful bath.

Pleasure and Resisting Pleasure

Physical pleasure is an experience which women with low body acceptance avoid. If you don't feel connected to your body, you are missing opportunities for juicy body feelings and sensations. Sometimes even women with good total self-esteem put off sybaritic, or sensual, body pleasure. One good way to start feeling a little more at ease is to take a pleasurable bath or shower. Let yourself relax and enjoy it. You deserve it.

A lot of us put a ceiling on pleasure: we start feeling anxious and uneasy when we begin to have too much success or when we feel too good. We have been taught to feel anxious if things go too well because our first job in life is to take care of others. If we are taking care of ourselves we may be neglecting our duties.

Those of us who have deficits in the area of body acceptance often deny ourselves pleasure in a variety of ways. One way is by refusing to buy any nice clothes, saying "I'm too fat to buy clothes. I have to wait until I lose ten pounds." If you do this, you should go out and buy yourself something comfortable and pretty, exotic or outrageous. This is not a superficial fix to make you look good on the outside, but a powerful meta-message from you to you that you are worthy of being treated like the unique jewel you are. Treating yourself badly by not wearing attractive clothes only makes the problem worse.

Exercise: Pleasure—Dressing for Self-Esteem Success

Buy yourself one article of clothing in a beautiful fabric. Make sure it's a color that pleases you and that you like the texture of. Buy something on sale or at a resale shop if you are feeling a financial pinch. Start slowly and allow yourself to enjoy a richly hued silk flower, a gossamer scarf, tie-dye socks, flowing velvet, soft cotton, or slinky rayon. Let yourself play dress-up and have some fun. This is just for you.

Exercise: Acting "As If"

If you find you have really strong objections to doing anything kind for yourself, try acting as if you didn't. If you are nervous and anxious, acting "as if" you are relaxed by doing deep breathing can create physiologic changes that actually produce feelings of relaxation and well-being. You can intervene in your own physiology to change how you feel.

If you are feeling out of sorts, remember a time when you laughed so hard your stomach hurt. Allow yourself, just for a moment, to set aside the way you feel right now and act as if you had just laughed your guts out. Let your smile widen and deepen, even dare to let yourself chuckle or snicker or laugh out loud. The truth is that you are not just pasting on a smile, but are allowing yourself to remember and create a different and more pleasurable state of being.

Do one nice thing for yourself today. Five minutes counts. Self-care is healthy selfishness. Treat yourself with some of the care you lavish on others. You can always go back to punishing yourself tomorrow. Of course, it will be much better when you are strong enough to resist punishing yourself at all. Punishing yourself always makes it more difficult for you to function well. It's time to stop the punishment and try something else.

Exercise: Restoring Yourself in the Bath

Women often deny themselves the pleasure of a leisurely bath. They believe it is frivolous or self-centered. Some women feel too anxious to take a bath; they need to begin with a foot bath and gradually work up to the full luxurious experience.

Sybaritic baths are one of the most effective ways to restore yourself in body, mind, and spirit. Immersion in warm to moderately hot water for twenty minutes does a number of good things. It improves circulation, taking nutrients where they are needed and assisting the elimination of toxins. It relaxes muscles so that tension from physical exertion or psychological stress is released. It encourages release of endorphins, so that you feel relaxed, content, happy, and optimistic. It rinses off positive ions you absorb from the wear and tear of living and replaces these stress-produced positive ions with feel-good negative ions. Finally, it provides a reparative, restorative experience where you can wash off and soak away the physical and emotional residue accumulated from your day.

Take a minimum of twenty minutes for a restorative bath. Put up the "Privacy Please" sign. Give your senses free rein: let your intuition guide your selection of sensory delights.

Experiment with:

1. Candles and music in your bathroom: soothing classical music, spicy salsa, sensual samba, evocative jazz;

2. Rose petals, slippery scented soaps, a few drops of an essential oil (rose oil for luxury, lavender oil for deep relaxation, rosemary or peppermint oil for energy);

3. A loofah (press gently), a real sea sponge (caressing, velvety), a body brush.

After your bath, try using some organic sesame seed oil. Massage the oil all over your body, starting with your face and neck and working your way down your body. Organic sesame seed oil is a natural anti-oxidant, which is absorbed by the skin within seconds. It provides immediate oxygen to cells and tissue. It attaches to the lipid receptor sites beneath the surface layer of the skin and counters or fights free radicals, keeping your body in healthy balance. In addition, an organic sesame seed oil massage followed by a bath or shower is an inexpensive effective remedy for dry skin (Chopra 1996).

Pleasure: Sexuality and Sensuality

Sexuality is initially a biologically driven function. Infants can and do have orgasms; physiology pushes them toward pleasurable release. As you grow up, a lot of what turns you on sexually is mediated by culture and learning. You are exposed to family and friends' preferences, to influences from authorities and peer groups at school, and to popular magazines, music, and television, all of which has an impact on your sexuality.

Specific sexual experiences can influence how you feel about your own sexuality as well. Hopefully your first experience was with a loving partner, and the experience infused you with a sense of joy about your own sexuality. If you were the victim of a sexual assault, you may have lingering feelings of guilt and shame even though you did nothing wrong.

The Reality

For most women, sexual experience is embedded in the content of relationship. Following the feminine script to be pleasing and compliant, women sometimes feel pressured to have sex in order to have a relationship. Sometimes we believe that nobody would really want us just for ourselves.

When we follow the feminine script, we sometimes assume that having sex means we are in a relationship that includes love and commitment. Our partner may not have made the same assumptions. Even when our partner says: "I'm not ready for a committed relationship," or "I want to date other people," or "I'm not getting along with my wife," sometimes we believe that if we are loving enough, caring enough, sensitive enough, perfect, we can make that other person really love us.

Following the feminine script, we sometimes fake orgasms to make the other person feel better. Sometimes we can't speak up when we don't really want sex and instead want affection or attention.

Improving Your Sexual Reality

Do the exercises in this book: they will help you develop better and better understanding of your needs, wants, desires, and preferences.

The exercises in this chapter will help you with body acceptance, and if you have body acceptance, your body will tell you everything else you need to know; when to eat, when to sleep, when to get out and boogey. It will also tell you about your own longing for affection, for touch, for sex, for deep connection. There are many wonderful things your body can give you, if you allow yourself to be connected. Your body is the basic encyclopedia of information about your feelings. You cannot accurately know what you feel without being aware of what is going on in your body.

If you are in body acceptance and in love, you may have an experience of being completely, totally in the moment. You are connecting with your whole being to the whole being of another person. You can be touching on many different levels. Your bodies are touching, your spirits are touching, your feelings are touching. You are totally merged into this deep connection with the person you love. The enjoyment of your sexuality can be a part of your love for another person.

If you like, sexual experience with yourself can bring enormous pleasure and soothing contentment. The important thing to know is that there is no one right way to approach sexuality. There are many choices. Each adult is responsible for making her own choice, which includes choosing abstinence.

Along with sexuality, there are the sensual pleasures, which are not necessarily sexual. Sensuality means the pleasures enjoyed by the body through the five senses; sensual pleasure is not genital arousal, it is softer and more subtle.

Exercise: Enhancing Your Sexuality and Sensuality

Embracing body acceptance enables you to be as alive and fully present as possible. You allow yourself to enjoy the sensual pleasures, many of which are restorative and enhancing. Try rubbing lotion on your body after a nice warm bath. You could do it quickly, in a mechanical way, just to get the job done. Or, you could do it in a slow, more enjoyable way, tuning in to your body. Think of a mommy rubbing lotion on her baby. Think of giving a friend a massage because her muscles are sore.

As a woman, you instinctively know how to make your baby, friend, or husband feel better. Yet most of us have a lot of trouble putting these skills into service for ourselves.

What we need to do is to wake up from the habitual patterns that keep us from getting in touch with our real selves. Try something different to get off automatic. If you always take a quick shower, this time close the door and have a bubble bath.

Rest: Why Women Find It Difficult to Get Adequate Rest

Getting an adequate amount of rest is very important for all women. Yet most women find it hard to get enough rest. Women have multiple jobs. Traditionally, we are the keepers of the home, the keepers of relationships, the ones who make everything at work go right. And it's women who generally keep the social date book, keep track of birthdays and anniversaries, write the cards, and keep in touch with all the relatives.

We have been taught since birth that relationships are our responsibility. This belief is so pervasive that we will not only have a good relationship with our bosses, co-workers, and friends, we will also have relationships with the seller at the newsstand, the cafeteria clerk who takes our money, and even with salespeople who badger us on the phone.

Men generally take a more businesslike approach to life. Men usually don't worry about what the cafeteria clerk thinks of them personally. They hand over the money and collect the change and they're on their way. But often a woman will stop and say, "How are you today?" or, "Let me see if I have the exact change," or, "The apple pie looks really good." Women are always busy relating to everyone. Keeping so many relationships going is work. It's exhausting.

Women don't realize how much effort and energy all these relationships require. There's an old saying, "A woman's work is never done." This constant expenditure of a woman's energy to support and nurture so many relationships can lead to exhaustion. Exhaustion can lead to stress, a short temper, forgetfulness, car accidents, and even physical symptoms such as headaches, backaches, sore shoulders and necks, nausea, flu, and on and on and on. Rest and recreation are absolutely necessary to keep a woman restored and functioning at her best, for herself and others.

There may be many reasons you avoid rest. If you are frantic, on a treadmill, constantly busy, you may be running away from your ability to enjoy life fully and deeply. If your feelings build and build in intensity, you may have ignored your needs for so long that a crisis develops.

We think we are not supposed to rest. We have absorbed this idea from culture. This belief is deeply rooted in most of us. Now is the time to change. You are probably saying, "I just can't find the time. There is no more time in my day."

Rest: Nancy's Story

Nancy's husband died suddenly of an unexpected heart attack. Nancy loved her husband deeply and the relationship was the result of a lot of hard work on both sides. After his death, she threw herself into working two jobs, going back to school, and taking care of her son. She kept herself frantically busy in an effort to avoid the pain of losing her beloved husband. Her health started to suffer; allergies, asthma, and chronic flu troubled her.

Nancy desperately needed rest. Her best friend, Melissa, sat Nancy down and lovingly told her that she thought Nancy was running herself into the ground. Melissa knew Nancy well enough to point out that her son couldn't afford to lose his only surviving parent.

One evening, after working all day, making dinner for her son, and attending an evening class, Nancy remembered her friend's concern. She walked across the street from her house and sat on a child's swing in the park. She said later, "You know, that was one of the hardest things I ever did. I had to force myself to go to the park, instead of starting another project. But I can hardly put into words the difference it made to have that half hour. It was like a miracle."

Exercise: Get Some Rest

Plan on taking fifteen minutes for yourself after dinner. Tell your husband or boyfriend or children, "I'm going to my room for fifteen minutes. Please don't interrupt me unless the house starts burning down." Hope they don't set it on fire.

Shut and lock the door, and take five deep breaths. Let the harried life outside the door continue without you. Shrug your shoulders and imagine that your problems and worries fall off. Don't read; reading can be a way to avoid connecting with yourself in the same way TV can. Listen to calming music, do some stretches. Take a fragrant bubble bath, or, if you hate baths, take a shower.

Don't be surprised if the internal critic clicks on and tries to hurry you. You may hear, "I shouldn't do this. I should fold the laundry. I'm wasting time." Beware of "shoulds" and "oughts." Tell that nagging voice to shut up. The last thing you need or deserve is self-criticism. You deserve quiet time for yourself.

Get out your self-esteem journal and take credit for taking a rest break. Write "rest break, fifteen minutes." The specifics are important. Squeeze the juice out of your rest break. Record your accomplishment and make another deposit in your self-esteem bank account.

Appearance

We all know that appearance (what you do with what you've got) is superficial. Yet, whether we like it or not, appearance is perceived as a significant determinant of self-esteem, a reflection of how you care for yourself. Your appearance sends a message to others about your self-esteem "What you see is what you get." Research has revealed that first impressions are powerful. They determine whether you'll get the job, close the deal, interest someone else in wanting to get to know you better.

Self-presentation is a message to you about your worth and a message to others about your investment in yourself. Overconcern with your physical appearance can be just as damaging as unconcern about your self-presentation. Some husbands have never seen their wives without full makeup. Pride in yourself is one thing, wearing a mask is another. This is a fragile coping mechanism. What happens if you age, get caught in a downpour, go swimming?

A lack of appropriate concern about self-presentation often conveys lack of self-awareness, lack of information, or contempt for others. "I don't need to do any of that because I feel so superior."

When You Can't Stand to Look at Yourself

You may hate looking at yourself in the mirror. You may have trained yourself to purposely look away whenever you walk by a reflecting store window or find yourself in an elevator with mirrored walls. You are determined not to look. However, you can't avoid the fact that how you see your body is a critical part of who you are.

Even more importantly, how you *feel* about your body is part of your core self-esteem. You may not be able to change much about the body you have inherited. But learning to take better care of your body can change how you feel about yourself. Caring *for* your body can lead to caring *about* your body and yourself.

Exercise: Look in the Mirror

If you hate to look at yourself in a mirror, take some private time and try it. Put on shorts and a short-sleeved top, or, if you can, strip down to nothing. Remember that many women hate their bodies. If you feel anxious, nervous, or upset by this idea, just let the feeling pass through you.

Your job is to be nonjudgmental and simply observe your own body and your feelings. If you can't look at your whole body, use a little mirror. Just look at one eye in the mirror, or look only from your knees down. Make friends with your feet. Feet are tremendously important—they hold the rest of you up!

Begin by giving yourself credit for any small positive detail you can find about your body. For instance, you might say, "I have nice eyes." "I like my little finger, it curves in sort of a graceful way." "The color of my hair is okay."

On any body, there is something to like. Find whatever small things you can and acknowledge them. It's a step toward acknowledging your whole body. The tiniest step counts.

If you think of yourself as overweight, you will increase your body acceptance by thinking of yourself as curvy and voluptuous. If you think of yourself as too skinny, you will increase your body acceptance by thinking of yourself as lean and lithe.

Remember that you don't have to do this or any exercise perfectly.

Perfection is never a reasonable goal. Perfectionist goal-setting actually sabotages performance.

Some of us have such badly damaged body images that we will be unable to do very much of this exercise. That's all right. Do what you can, and, at some later time, try again. You don't have to do it perfectly. Give yourself written credit in your self-esteem journal for completing the smallest part of this exercise. Congratulate yourself for confronting your demons. Every little bit counts.

Women Who Are Obsessed With Their Looks

You may be on the other end of the spectrum; you may look in the mirror obsessively. If so, you may be using your body to cover up how you really feel about yourself. You may say to yourself, "My makeup looks good, therefore everything in my life is okay," even though that's not true. "I look good" does not always mean "I feel good." In this instance, you are looking at your outer beauty in order to avoid facing inner emotions that you don't know how to handle. You are checking to make sure your flaws are hidden, invisible to others, making sure that the disguise is intact. Even though you are able to look at yourself in the mirror, you are not in a healthy state of body acceptance.

Exercise: How to Stop the Obsession

If you can't seem to stop looking at yourself, change your experience a little. Make a temporary rule, even for one hour or one day, that you will only look in the mirror once in the morning, once at noon, and once at night. Give yourself a big cheer when you resist compulsive looking. This is your path to finding out that there is a lot more to you than what's on the outside. Once you know how to plumb the depths of your inner self you will be able to find real jewels of strength, endurance, honesty, creativity, and even compassion for yourself.

Time for Yourself

When you follow the feminine script, you often work full-time, caring for others. When you understand more about what nourishes your own self-esteem, from which you nurture everyone else, you may realize that you need time for yourself. You understand that time for yourself is an absolute necessity, not a luxury.

Exercise: Your Cheerleading Squad

The purpose of this exercise is to help you feel supported, encouraged, loved and appreciated, even when there is no one available to provide these things for you. You deserve to have your own cheering squad. After all, you are cheering others on all the time. You can have anyone you want on your cheering squad. Think big! You might want your cheering squad to include your favorite celebrities or writers. You can have anyone you want, from Michael J. Fox to Oprah, from Celine Dion to Princess Diana. Add your favorite friends, parents, and colleagues to your squad.

Now let your cheering squad create a fabulous cheer for you. It might go like this:

> You are the center of beauty and life, your destiny's not pain and strife. You are strong, vibrant and free, you can be anything you want to be. We are behind you 100 percent, you will never be broken or bent. Go girl, go, we're right behind, the future you've got is blowing your mind. Go, go, go, go, go, go, go, you can't be stopped, that you know.

Write out your cheer. Imagine your cheerleaders grooving to the rhythm of your special cheer. Enjoy. You could even put your cheer on tape and listen to it when the need arises.

Exercise: How to Negotiate Time for Yourself

Unless you get enough rest and restoration, you are not going to be the brilliant, clear-thinking, able-bodied woman you want to be. In a larger sense, this is not something you're doing only for yourself. You restore yourself so you can be the best you can be for yourself and others. You want to be a woman who models appropriate self-care for your children, spouse, friends, bosses, and co-workers.

As you start to change the situation, take small steps. Start really small. Assign a few chores. Say, "Tomorrow night, Jessica is going to do the dishes and Brandon is going to sweep the floor." Ask your husband to come to your assistance. Figure out one or two things that he could be in charge of every night. Maybe you can negotiate one night a week that is guaranteed to you for self-care. Your free night could be spent in any way you want: out with a friend or by yourself at a movie or the library or a book club, or at home taking some time for yourself.

When you let your family and friends know you are exhausted, you may find channels of communication opening up. Some women who have tried this have been surprised at how willing their family was to help them. You may find that your family is grateful that you are willing to talk to them about being so exhausted. All too often, we continue in our own little shells, not asking for help and not expecting any. Making better connections with your family by being realistic about your needs may be one of the additional benefits of trying to get enough rest for yourself. A calm, restored woman is of much better use and more enjoyable to everyone than a woman who is edgy, deprived, and burdened.

CHAPTER 4

Acquiring the Courage to Feel

When you follow the feminine script, you appear to be happy, optimistic, cheerful, interested, and patient. You may be presenting a false self to the world and to yourself, hiding the full truth about your feelings. You may sometimes feel angry, sad, hurt, scared, disappointed, envious, helpless, anxious, defective, and ashamed for having "negative" feelings. Unable to feel good all the time, you may hide some of your feelings, even from yourself, and frequently from others, until you fall into anger or irritation or depression. When you can't identify and cope positively with your feelings in daily life, your vitality becomes depleted and your self-esteem is eroded.

You may sometimes feel excited, content, sexy, proud, and confident, but these feelings may seem too intense or not ladylike. You may believe that you can't express these feelings without looking conceited. Yet, not being able to laugh from your belly or express your most outrageous dreams of success puts a damper on your ability to be your most authentic and powerful.

Experts on human development have emphasized the adaptive importance of the ability to experience the full range of feelings in healthy human functioning, even though some of the feelings themselves may feel toxic and horrible (Masterson 1988). When you suppress negative feelings you also diminish your ability to feel positive feelings. In order to feel joy, excitement, love, curiosity, satisfaction, and contentment, you must also be willing to feel anger, sadness, disappointment, hurt, envy, shame, and fear. To feel less than fully is to mute the emotional music which is essential to being completely alive.

What's in It for You

Knowing exactly what you feel is critical information for your survival and for being as happy, satisfied, and creative as you can be. Learning how to identify specific feelings and how to cope with uncomfortable feelings puts you in the driver's seat. Instead of careening out of control (too angry, too depleted, too confused), you can learn how to map your feeling states and make a plan for how to deal with specific feelings. Developing high-level skills for coping with feelings allows you more freedom, more power, more control over your own destiny.

The Importance of Acknowledging All Feelings

We have enormous resistance to experiencing the entire range of our feelings. We want to get rid of the ugly feelings of envy, anger, shame, and fear. Yet emotional access to ourselves is not a switch we can turn on when the feeling is good and off when the feeling is bad. When we inhibit the "bad" feeling states, we also constrict the "good" feeling states.

In order to have healthy self-esteem, we have to be able to acknowledge the wide range of feelings that are part of the human experience.

The process of learning to acknowledge the entire range of feelings takes courage. It requires courage to admit that you are jealous and want what another person has. Only through acknowledging jealousy and learning to reduce the intensity of it can you prevent the feeling from spilling out onto another person or poisoning you. Feeling jealous, but not aware that you are, you might comment to a friend, "That outfit is great. Don't you think it would look better on your daughter?" Your comment, which first gives a compliment and then takes it away, is your attempt to get rid of your jealous feeling by taking your friend down a notch, making yourself feel superior in the moment.

You might also turn your unacknowledged, unnamed feeling of jealousy in on yourself. Maybe you admired how your friend looked, felt jealous and inferior, and then attacked yourself. "I'm too fat and I'll never be as thin as Debbie. I don't really deserve anything because I did this to myself."

Some feelings have a bad reputation because they are physiologically unpleasant, or because we don't know how to cope with them without hurting ourselves or someone else. It is difficult to know how to handle the darker feelings of anger, jealousy, fear, and disgust. It is distressing to feel betrayed or to have your pride wounded or to be sad. The recognition and appropriate handling of anger is difficult for most women. We often don't know when we are feeling angry or resentful.

If you don't know how to identify your feelings or how to make positive use of them, don't blame yourself. Our culture doesn't stress these skills, and we are fortunate if we somehow learned skills for dealing with negative feelings when we were growing up.

Many of us have difficulty expressing negative feelings to others because we are afraid that to give voice to our real feelings may threaten our relationships. In the women's training program, we learn to please others, to be attuned to the feelings of others, and to put others' welfare before our own. We fear that if we speak up about our real feelings they will be dismissed, ignored, ridiculed, or abandoned: "If I am my real self, no one will like me or love me."

Sometimes, feelings of joy, excitement, pleasure, and feeling free and spontaneous are also experienced as dangerous. If you grew up in a dysfunctional family you may have learned to fear pleasure. Pleasure wasn't permitted in your family, so you now believe it's dangerous to feel too good for very long. You may experience a ceiling on pleasure. If you feel too good for very long you become anxious, believing that something bad is going to happen.

What Happens When You Feel

As women, we are taught to believe that various aspects of ourselves are disconnected and function separately. The truth is, we are all unified beings: body, brain, heart, mind, and spirit. All these parts function together and interact constantly. A broken arm affects not only your body but your brain, heart, mind, and spirit as well. With a broken arm, you may feel irritation, frustration, and anger because of the additional difficulties in functioning. You may feel fear and anxiety about being able to care for your children and yourself, and being able to function adequately in your job. You may feel discouraged, depressed, and hopeless if your broken arm is a complicated fracture with a protracted healing time.

The Positive Uses of All Feeling States

Because we as women need to learn how to make more positive use of our feelings, we need to understand how intense emotion affects our entire being. *All negative feelings have the potential to be useful when we learn to understand and cope with them.* Anger and rage can be used to create appropriate boundaries, limits, and protection for ourselves and those we love. Perhaps if more people had let themselves feel hatred, Hitler would have been stopped sooner. Hurt, sadness, and vulnerability can deepen our ability to connect with and understand our own past histories, offering ourselves increased compassion and empathy. Sadness and hurt can also allow us deeper and closer relationships with others. We can identify with another's sadness or hurt and feel more connected to them.

Improving our ability to experience and use negative feelings enriches our capacity to feel the positive ones. Clearing out anger, resentment, hurt, and sadness opens the door to feeling satisfaction, joy, excitement, and wonder. Identifying, acknowledging, and learning to cope with all feeling states, even the ones that are noxious, allows us to become more vital.

Our Emotional Landscape

Our feeling states can be divided into three categories. *Passionate feelings* (anger, rage, fear, envy, jealousy) produce hyper-arousal in our minds and bodies. Anxiety is a variant of fear and shares the same physiology. When we have passionate feelings, we are buffeted by an internal storm of agitation—strong emotion that pushes to be released. Our hearts pound, our blood boils, and we want to take action to get relief from the internal earthquake (Goleman 1995.)

Softer feelings (sadness, vulnerability, hurt, confusion, and depression) produce hypo-arousal in our minds and bodies. We collapse into ourselves, stuck in an emotional quicksand. Our heart rate slows, blood moves to the center of our bodies, blood pressure drops, we often feel cold. We want to withdraw into ourselves. Everything grinds to a halt (Goleman 1995.)

Mild to moderate anxiety and depression are a natural part of life. However, chronic anxiety, panic attacks, and chronic deep depression are *disordered feeling states*. These disordered feeling states are attempts to cope with intense emotional pain. Disordered feeling states are biochemical in nature. We may have a genetic or constitutional vulnerability to becoming chronically anxious or panicky or severely depressed. If you notice that you experience chronic anxiety, panic attacks, or severe depression which interferes with your functioning, know that it is not your fault. If you try to work things out on your own and don't experience relief within a reasonable amount of time, you may need professional help (a physician or mental health professional) to give you the assistance you need to feel better.

The Passionate Feelings

Imagine this scenario: Your eight year-old daughter has been sitting in the living room with her suitcase for the last two hours, waiting for her father to pick her up for a scheduled overnight visitation. She is sad, hurt, and anxious. You are angry. The first half hour, you were worried that maybe his car broke down or he got stuck in traffic. You tried to reach him at home, at his office, and on his cell phone. You couldn't connect.

Now, your heart is beating faster, your blood pressure is up, adrenaline is pumping, and your muscles are tense. You are ready to do battle. Your body, brain, heart, mind, and spirit are all interacting to prepare you to deal with this situation in the best way to help your daughter. The first intense surge of anger has passed, and you know you need to calm yourself so that you can comfort your daughter. Your brain and body begin to relax their state of hyper-arousal. You help your daughter talk about her disappointment. You let her know she is a wonderful girl and that it's not her fault her dad hasn't come.

The other passionate feelings work the same way. Something triggers fear, anxiety, rage, envy, or jealousy, and your whole being leaps into readiness for flight or fight. You are zooming down a familiar freeway route to pick up your husband after work. Looking up, you see a string of red taillights flash on. Startled, you grind to a halt, inches from the car in front of you. Your quick reaction saves your life. Your sense organs (eyes, ears, nose, and skin) react to the triggering event and send information to your brain, which puts you on alert. You scan the environment for more information. Your mind races to figure out if there is real danger. All this happens within a few seconds. After the initial rush, which is very brief, there is a second, longer surge through your whole being. This results in hyper-vigilance, which enables you to get more information.

At times like this, you need to be able to reduce the intensity of your feelings to allow you to think more clearly. If you need help with this, you should try some of the self-soothing techniques covered in the next chapter.

The Softer Feelings

You and your husband have just separated. You feel devastated. Your hands and feet are cold. You feel wave after wave of sadness—you can't believe anything can be this painful. You have a hard time getting out of bed. You can't imagine how you are going to get through this. You have to avoid all the places the two of you used to go. You feel ashamed. You had put heart and soul into being your real self in this relationship, warts and all. You have a feeling this is your fault—after all, it *is* the job of women to fix relationships.

You know that you have to pull yourself together and go on. You talk with a close friend about the incredible pain you are feeling. It seems you can't even do the basics. You feel so depressed that you don't have any energy. Your friend listens with understanding and without judgment. She is wise and knows you have to get yourself moving in order to feel better. She suggests the two of you take a walk. She understands that physical movement, even five or ten minutes, can begin to change your depressed physiology. She also suggests the two of you rent a sad movie, so you can sob your guts out.

You know that moving through the deep grief of your loss will take time. You begin to feel more hopeful with your friend's help. Exercise, taking extra good care of yourself, and other self-soothing and self-activation techniques (see chapter 5, "Getting Off the Emotional Tightrope") can make an enormous difference in feeling better more quickly, even though this process of healing takes time.

The Feeling Intensity Scale

You can gauge the intensity of any feeling by using a simple 0–10 scale. Zero is having none of the feeling, and 10 is having the maximum amount. The feeling intensity scale allows you to figure out how you are doing emotionally before you go over the edge into blasting anger, leaking frustration and irritation, making mean comments, falling into depression, or skyrocketing with anxiety. It helps you feel calmer, more able to cope. Any feeling can be plugged into the scale: anger, fear, envy, sadness, hurt, joy, excitement, confusion.

Learning to use the feeling intensity scale allows you to know more clearly how intense your emotions are and which feelings are most problematic for you. Knowing the intensity of any feeling allows you to figure out how close you are to blowing up, flaking out, giving in, or making a mess of things. It's like buying insurance for your safety, well-being, and happiness.

Sometimes Even Positive Feelings Can Be Dangerous

You may think that only negative feelings like anger, sadness, or hurt need to be monitored on the feeling intensity scale. But sometimes the positive feelings of excitement or curiosity or sexual arousal can get you into trouble.

Take the feeling of excitement. Excitement feels good. You associate it with feeling happy and eager and stimulated. You might think that it would be impossible to be *too* excited. That's not true. For example, what if you were excited about the prospect of buying a new car. You were so excited that when you went into the dealership a slick salesman convinced you that an old clunker with nice lines was the car for you. The salesman got you to sign a lease charging you more money than the car was really worth. Not until hours later, when you were at home with the signed papers in hand, did you realize you had been foolish. You realize that feeling a 9 on a scale of excitement was not such a good idea when buying a car.

Another example of a good feeling that might be dangerous is sexual arousal. If you are in a committed relationship with a healthy partner, getting to a 9 on the intensity of sexual arousal can be a wonderful thing. But if you go into a bar and meet a stranger and reach an 8 or a 9, sexual arousal is *not* a good thing. This person could be dangerous or have a sexually transmitted disease. But when your arousal is high, your thinking skills are impaired. You are out of control and could make a terrible decision. You need to learn how to identify the intensity of any feeling so you can use that information in a helpful proactive way. Once you learn how to identify the intensity of your sexual arousal, you will know to eighty-six yourself from the bar as soon as you reach a 4 on the 0–10 scale.

Exercise: Learning How to Travel Up and Down the Emotional Richter Scale

The purpose of this exercise is to teach you how to identify exactly where you are on the feeling intensity scale. You will practice with the feeling of anger, but you can repeat the exercise using any feeling you wish.

Description of the feeling intensity scale. Think about anger. On the 0–10 scale, a 0 is no anger at all. One is feeling a tiny amount of irritation. At a 3 or 4 on the scale, you notice that your breathing is more rapid. You may notice tension in your arms and hands, a tightness in your chest, a flushed warm feeling in your face, neck, and chest. You may feel tense and agitated, like you want to do something, but it's not exactly clear what to do to feel better. As the intensity of the anger increases, you begin to feel more and more uncomfortable. At a 6 or 7 on the scale, you may be pacing, raising your voice, beginning to sweat. At a 9 or 10 on the scale you feel explosive, out of control.

Practicing with the Feeling Intensity Scale. Right now, let yourself remember or imagine a time when you were at a 1 on the scale of anger—a time when you felt just a trace of mild irritation. Notice what that feeling of very mild, just noticeable irritation is like for you. Notice and observe what comes into your mind when you feel this mild irritation. Observe the physical sensations in your body. Notice your breathing.

Now travel up the scale to a 4. Remember or imagine a time when you felt moderately angry. Observe the feelings and sensations in your body. Notice your breathing. Notice the tension in your muscles. Notice if you feel flushed, hot, or if you are beginning to sweat.

Now, go up the scale to a 7. Let yourself remember and imagine feeling very angry. Notice your breathing. Notice the tension in your body. Observe exactly where the tension is and what it feels like. Notice the tension in your face and jaw muscles. Notice the tension in your hands. Notice the heat in your arms, hands, and chest.

Just as you traveled up the scale of intensity, you should now allow yourself to travel back down the scale to the point where you feel no anger. Take a few deep breaths and return to 0.

Being authentically human means being able to experience a wide spectrum of feelings. You have faced them, you have known them to be part of yourself, and ideally you have come to some sort of reckoning with them. We humans are like a rich tapestry with threads of all the emotions woven into us in complex and variable ways. This is the truth of being human.

Exercise: Comforting Yourself When You Feel Terrible

This exercise is meant to help you feel more calm and centered. It is what your best friend or caring parent would say to comfort you when you are feeling terrible.

Read the next three paragraphs to yourself until you begin to feel calmer. You could also put them on a tape and listen to the soothing words.

"I'm not letting go of my past. My past has helped me be who I am today. What I am doing is neutralizing my toxic and painful feelings from the past. I need to embrace my past and know it deeply, completely, and fully in order to free myself from the old, repetitive, self-destructive patterns of behavior which allow me to cherish the false belief that if I had only been better, my parents would have loved me for myself.

"What happened in the past cannot be changed—I cannot change the character of my parents, my children, or anyone else—that job is theirs and theirs alone. What I can do is let go of my toxic feelings and the belief that I must have been bad because other people mistreated me.

"The truth is, there is no one like me in this world. I have my own special and unique talents, gifts, and abilities. There is no one who can do a better job of being me than I can. Even if I don't know what it is, I have been given a life purpose. If I don't know my purpose right now, I need to allow it to emerge into my awareness in order to be my most peaceful, satisfied, complete self."

The Feeling Checklist

Knowing exactly what you feel is essential in order to connect with your core of vitality and energy. Knowing what you feel can protect you and others from destructive and corrosive behaviors, which can leak out when you are not conscious of your deepest real feelings. If you know you are depressed, you can decide to consult a professional. You can communicate to your family and friends that you are depressed, which helps them not to personalize it and to be more understanding and helpful to you. If you feel angry and frustrated about how your boss is treating you, you can let your husband and children know that your frustration is about your job and not about them.

Sometimes you may feel generally awful or bad, experiencing free-floating anxiety or dread. Learning to identify the specific emotions which underlie this general feeling is your pathway to freedom. As you learn to scan your inner experience to uncover your real feelings, use the *feeling checklist* (as illustrated) to help you identify specific feeling states. Feeling "awful" doesn't tell you very much. But feeling "sad," or "annoyed," or "frustrated" is specific and can tell you a lot. Knowing exactly what you feel is a crucial clue to solving the mystery of your own discomfort.

It's not always easy to know what you feel. You have to become a detective in order to figure it out. For example, when we say we are angry, a little detective work shows that ninety percent of the time our anger is really a reaction to another feeling such as hurt, sadness, or fear. Anger often functions as a distraction from the pain of the deeper feelings because it allows you to feel tough and strong. When you feel the softer feelings, you may feel vulnerable and helpless.

The feeling checklist provides a mini-container in which to put your feelings. Sometimes you may interpret your feelings as wild, even dangerous, and turn off or shut down your feelings. Be careful if you suspect you are in flight from your feelings. Drinking, working too much, taking drugs, sleeping, binge eating, driving fast, exercising compulsively, and picking up sex partners indiscriminately are unhealthy options. The first step in dealing with your feelings is simply to name them. Learn what they are. It is true that once you accurately name a feeling, it often loses much of its power over you.

Exercise: The Feeling Checklist

Become an expert in knowing what you feel. Correct identification of your feelings will allow you to make more effective choices about how to cope with a particular feeling. Using the feeling checklist will help you to become aware of all your feelings, provide a place to express that you had a specific feeling, and allow you to look for patterns (e.g., you always feel sad and never angry, you frequently feel angry or frustrated and rarely feel vulnerable).

Use the feeling checklist at the end of every day. Go down the list and find the feeling you are having right now. Let's say it's "sad." Put a check mark next to sad. Then ask yourself, "On a scale of 1 to

10, how sad am I?" Just a little bit sad? Mark 3 in the column. Fill in your checklist every day and mark every feeling you have experienced that day. Add to the list of feelings with your own words to describe feelings that you experience. Notice how rich and deep your emotional experience becomes after a week of using the feeling checklist.

Feeling Checklist

Feeling	Mon.	Tues.	Wed.	Thurs.	Fri.	Sat.	Sun.
Week of:							
Abandoned							
Afraid							
Angry							
Anxious							
Ashamed							
Betrayed							
Bored							
Calm							
Concerned							
Confused							
Contemptuous							
Content							
Disappointed							
Disgusted							
Embarassed							
Envious							
Excited							
Forgiving							
Grateful							
Happy							
Helpless							
Hopeful							
Hopeless							
Humiliated							
Hurt							
Insecure							
Jealous							
Joyous							
Lonely							
Optimistic							

Overwhelmed						
Peaceful						
Proud						
Relaxed						
Resentful						
Sad						
Scared						
Self-hatred						
Self-loathing						
Self-pity						
Sexy						
Suicidal						
Terrified						
Tired						
Trusting						
Vulnerable						
Worried						

CHAPTER 5

Getting Off the Emotional Tightrope

Getting into an intense storm of feelings is scary. Anxiety over taking a test, an attack of rage at your husband or children, frustrations at work: these intense emotions can cause you to burst into tears, feel sick to your stomach, or want to throw things. When you are upset and out of balance, you need better techniques to restore your emotional equilibrium, so you can feel better quickly.

Emotional balance is the ability to restore calm when you are upset, get going when you are in a slump, and retain a capacity to think even in the face of intense emotions. Emotional balance lets you know when you are vulnerable to losing control. It helps you know how to bring yourself back from the edge. It allows you to have a healthy relationship with your emotional life. You need to create a good alliance with your emotions, so that your feelings can inform your decisions.

We can all be overtaken by outbursts of primitive feelings. In those moments we feel possessed, and our ability to view our problems objectively is paralyzed. We need to balance ourselves internally, and that is an art which requires practice and skill. In this chapter, you will be shown how to clarify your feeling states and how to monitor your feelings, so you can self-regulate before you lose control. By learning a wide range of self-restoring techniques, you will enhance your ability to cope with your emotional self. This directly enhances your self-esteem, as you restore a sense of competence by being in charge of your feelings, rather than having your feelings be in charge of you.

Nicole's Story

Nicole, a tenth-grader, was suspended from school for three days because of a wild outburst in class. She screamed at her English teacher, threw her books to the ground, and stormed out of the room. She drove off, and was stopped by police twenty miles away for speeding. This was not the first time. Almost every week Nicole exploded into some kind of destructive behavior, driving erratically around town, sobbing loudly, and creating scenes at her friends' homes, even threatening to kill herself.

Nicole lacked skills for calming herself. So when something bad happened to her, she had no effective way to cope. She would be overcome by anger, hurt, sadness, or fear, and with no way to soothe herself, her feelings would escalate.

It's important to go back and look at exactly what made Nicole angry. On the surface, she was mad at the English teacher, but internally Nicole was angry with herself. She had not done the required schoolwork. Feelings of shame, guilt, anger, and worthlessness overwhelmed her. Her self-esteem plummeted to a low point. She couldn't stand how she felt inside, so she exploded to rid herself of her bad feelings.

Nicole would lose control of herself at least one night a week, usually after having a fight with her boyfriend. For example, one night her boyfriend said he wanted to break up with her. This was devastating. She called all three of her close girlfriends, but no one was home. She lacked the capacity to handle her feelings, so once again, she vented the bad feelings through her behavior. She drove to the home of an older boy, got drunk, and went out thrill-driving. They had sex, which only escalated her sense of shame and degradation. Eventually the police found her passed out in her car and took her home.

Nicole is sixteen years old. She has few inner resources. No one has ever taught her how to calm herself when she becomes upset.

Although Nicole is an extreme case, many of us—adults as well as young girls—have trouble coping with intense feelings. With no way to soothe ourselves, these feelings can create whirlwinds of emotion that push us over the edge.

Achieving emotional balance is critically related to achieving healthy self-esteem. When we gain our emotional balance, we get our feet on the ground. We are stabilized. We can go on with our lives confidently.

Why We Need to Strike a Balance Between Thinking and Feeling

It is critical to achieve a balance between thinking and feeling in order to make fully informed decisions. Too much emphasis on thinking can lead to devitalized living, an internal sense of impoverishment, stagnation in a dead-end job or a workaholic lifestyle. Too much emphasis on feelings can lead to impulsive decision-making, resulting in damaged relationships and poor judgment on the job and at home.

For most women, knowing their core feeling states and regulating them can be difficult for many reasons. Unidentified feelings often collapse into sludgy, dark, unfocused depression. A woman might say, "I'm tired. I'm depressed. I don't know why." She might blame her depressed feeling on her job, or her husband, or some circumstance in her life, without ever digging up the real interior feelings causing her depression.

Anger is often a disguise worn by more vulnerable feelings, such as sadness, hurt, and fear. When we feel angry, we often feel strong and powerful. Therefore, we come to prefer being angry over feeling other emotions. If our real feeling is hurt, but we respond instead with anger, we may harm others through projection and blame. Cycles of misunderstanding can skyrocket.

We tend to characterize the feelings of anxiety, worry, sadness, frustration, hurt, disappointment, fear, shame, helplessness, and isolation as "bad" feelings. These feelings are unpleasant, sometimes intolerable. Unconsciously, we may conclude, like we did as children, that if we *feel* this bad we must *be* this bad. But it's important to note that *there is nothing intrinsically bad about any feeling*. We call some feelings "bad" because we don't know how to deal with them. They become bad when we act them out in negative and destructive ways.

Even positive feeling states, such as joy, excitement, sexual arousal, simple well-being, and pride, can lead to problems when we react impulsively and do things that are bad for us (see chapter 4). If we lose our ability to balance thinking and feeling we may pay the price in guilt and a lessened sense of self.

Nicole's Story, Continued

Learning to name, decode, and peel off the layers of her feelings was of great help to Nicole. Once she learned how to use the feelings intensity scale, she was able to intervene in the moment between feeling bad and doing something out of control. She learned to get out her checklist and measure how much she was feeling a particular emotion: confused, 5, angry, 6, fearful, 10. The simple recognition of what her feelings were helped her to calm down.

Sarah's Story

Sarah, a thirty-year-old dermatologist, was great at her work but unable to function without her boyfriend Brad. Knowing she was totally dependent on him, he would provoke her by threatening to leave her. Sometimes he would hang up on her or drive away without her. Whenever this happened, she would call all their mutual friends and leave histrionic voicemails asking if they'd seen him; she would even get in her car and drive around town trying to find him.

Sarah desperately needed to understand what was really going on inside her. She knew her behavior with her boyfriend was out of line. She put up with Brad's controlling behavior, because she believed she had to in order to have any relationship at all. It was only a matter of time before she couldn't take any more abuse. She screamed at Brad, ranting and raving about his abusive treatment of her. She felt completely justified in her outrage and hysteria. She had to learn to break through that response.

Sarah realized that her reaction to her boyfriend's behavior was irrational. She only behaved in that way when she was in a state of intense fear and desperation. She needed a way to interrupt the intensity of her feeling states, so she could use her good thinking skills.

Shortly after Christmas, she was hysterical because Brad had promised to come over on Christmas Day, and he didn't come. By now Sarah was in therapy. She learned how to chart her feelings on the feeling intensity scale. When she charted her feelings this time, she realized she was at an 8 or 9 on the scale of anxiety, agitation, and fear. She recognized that she was not thinking clearly. She did some deep breathing, then stood to stretch her arms and legs. This small intervention helped tremendously in calming her down. She was now able to stand back a bit and look at her situation objectively. She saw that her fears were irrational. She was not going to die over the loss of contact with Brad. She was being driven by feelings from childhood which had traveled forward into the present. They were very real feelings, but they were feelings from her childhood.

As she continued her deep breathing, Sarah was able to see that she was still acting as though she were a little girl. Sarah's basic fear was of abandonment. When she was nine, her father went to work one day, had a heart attack, and died. Sarah still remembered coming home from school and waiting for her parents, who never came. Finally, someone remembered the little girl and an aunt came and took Sarah to her mother. Unfortunately, her mother was emotionally devastated and was unable to nurture her.

Sarah began to realize that any situation that triggered abandonment feelings was problematic for her. She felt, at some level, that she was being left out because she was bad and unworthy. She had lashed out, trying to connect with her boyfriend, in an attempt to get rid of her intolerable feelings.

In therapy Sarah expanded her healthy selfishness so that she felt more deserving of a good relationship. She gave her boyfriend a reasonable amount of time to change his behavior. When he didn't, Sarah started dating other people. Her self-esteem had improved so that she didn't have to stay in a bad relationship to feel good about herself.

Abandonment

Many people have issues of abandonment. It is not necessary for a parent to die for a child to feel abandoned. Children can feel abandoned when a parent is ill, depressed, or hospitalized. They can feel abandoned when a sibling has asthma or a serious surgery and the bulk of the parental resources are channeled into keeping the debilitated brother or sister alive and well.

All children experience moments of abandonment, moments of shame and humiliation, moments when they feel their survival is at risk. Here is a partial list of abandonment feelings: anger, rage, irritation, frustration, sadness, hurt, disappointment, fear, terror, vulnerability, anxiety, helplessness, isolation, fear of death. These feelings do not necessarily point only to abandonment; they could also be related to other issues. Learning to regulate your feelings is an important step on the path to deeper understanding of yourself.

As adults we need to regulate intense feelings. Using the feeling intensity scale described in chapter 4 can help. The next time you feel upset, stop and quickly chart yourself. At 2 or 3, you're okay. But program yourself so that a big warning signal goes off at 5. If your feeling state goes above a 5, stop. Move back from whatever you're doing. Don't say anything more. Take a time-out. Go into a room by yourself, or go home, but don't continue on the destructive path of intense emotion. Turn to the end of this chapter and utilize one of the self-regulating exercises.

If you are experiencing a passionate feeling (anger, fear, rage, envy, jealousy, anxiety) use one of the self-soothing techniques that follow to calm your emotional storm and restore emotional balance. If you are experiencing a softer feeling (sadness, vulnerability, hurt, confusion, depression) use one of the self-activation techniques to pull out of your slump.

The first step is measuring your feeling and recognizing you are heading up the emotional Richter scale. You want to avoid a major emotional blowout that may cause you trouble and bring pain to others. What you need to do is make the unpleasant feeling less intense. You have to intervene physiologically; in other words, help your body out of its pattern.

Giving Voice

While some of us have trouble controlling anger, others of us have trouble giving voice to our feelings. Some of us call our husband or friends and talk about something terrible that happened. But many of us try so hard to be perfect that we are unable to reach out to others in this way. Talking about a problem is one way to start dealing with it. It is not a sign of weakness to call a friend and say, "My boss just screamed at me in front of the whole staff about my project not being done. I feel so embarrassed I could die."

When you hold in worries and concerns, your anxiety can escalate; the problem gets bigger and bigger and bigger until it seems unsolvable. *Catastrophizing* is imagining that absolutely everything is going to go wrong and there is nothing you can do about it. There is no way out.

We have probably all had experiences with catastrophizing. It is not pleasant. When you are worrying at level 10 on the feeling intensity scale, you are catastrophizing. You need to find a way to stop and calm yourself.

An intense grief reaction can make us go off the chart. When Valerie's mother died six months ago, Valerie was gripped by irrevocable sadness and couldn't get on with her life. One of her first responses was binge eating, which made her feel even worse. Then her internal critic turned on her for being sad and for being fat. The internal critic kept telling her, "Get over it. Stop wallowing in self-pity." Valerie had to step back and find her feelings in order to move on. She had to acknowledge the reality of her intense grief and anger over her loss. She found help in a group at church for people going through the grieving process. In this group, she had a safe place to give voice to her sadness and loss.

Sometimes, the flight up the feeling intensity scale happens when you look in the mirror and hate what you see. You look puffy and out of shape. Your pants feel too tight. The internal critic kicks in and tells you that you have no willpower and will always be fat. You decide to go on a stringent diet, beginning immediately, and rid yourself of this disgusting flab once and for all. Panicking from overanticipation of the coming deprivation, you first treat yourself to a hot fudge sundae.

What you need to do is recognize that you are in the midst of an intense emotional tornado, and you need to soothe yourself in a way that doesn't make you feel worse. One immediate positive choice might be to call a friend who has been successful at getting into shape, and ask for her advice. Being humane to yourself when you feel disgusted by your own body takes enormous energy and a lot of work.

On the road to achieving healthy self-esteem, it's important to be able to stop and figure out what your feelings are. The closer you get to your deepest feelings, the more you enhance self-knowledge, self-compassion, and self-integration.

Recognizing Loss of Emotional Balance

It is natural and unavoidable in life to fall out of emotional balance at times. Parenting an infant interrupts your sleep and makes extraordinary demands on your ability to regulate yourself. Inadequate parenting early in your life may have left you with emotional vulnerability, similar to the original feelings of being abandoned or traumatized. These old feelings can resurface later in life.

Raising adolescents, caring for aging parents, or experiencing chronic illness or the loss of a job or a relationship can catapult you into emotional crises. Because of the developmental and situational pressures inherent in life, you fall out of emotional balance. In order to be the best you can be in difficult circumstances, you are faced with the need to retrieve, and restore that balance.

Self-Activation and Self-Soothing Techniques

You can use self-activation and self-soothing techniques to intervene directly in the intensity of your feelings. They allow you to experience quick physiologic and emotional relief. You can then think through your options and select the choice that is right for you.

Self-soothing techniques are designed to calm the passionate feelings of anger, rage, jealousy, envy, and fear. Self-soothing techniques can also be used to reduce the milder versions of the passionate feelings, such as irritation, frustration, and anxiety. Self-soothing techniques can help you when you can't stand one more stress, when you notice that your ability to think is in the toilet because you are so stirred up.

Self-activation techniques are needed when you experience the softer feelings, when you feel overwhelmed, depressed, vulnerable, sad, hurt, helpless, or confused. The self-activation techniques can help you on a day when you can't imagine how you're going to get out of bed and do what has to be done. Self-activation techniques can move you along when you feel stuck in emotional quicksand and lethargic, with no energy, like an engine without fuel.

Self-soothing and self-activation techniques are wonderfully effective because a minimum investment of time produces noticeable results quickly. These techniques intervene in the disruptive physiology that characterizes intense feeling states, providing immediate relief to your body, mind, and emotions. To make the best use of these techniques, try them out now. Don't wait for an emergency. The techniques will work in emergencies, but they will work better the more you are familiar with them.

Techniques for Relieving Both the Passionate Feelings and the Softer Feelings

The following two techniques are for reducing the intensity of both the passionate feelings and the softer feelings.

Exercise 1: The Container

1. While sitting comfortably in a chair, imagine a container that is about two feet away from you. Imagine the container in

three-dimensional space. Imagine the color and texture of the container. See the container in great detail.

2. Select a feeling you want to feel less of. Take 70 percent of that feeling (anger, fear, anxiety, helplessness, sadness) and transfer the feeling into the container, as you count from one to three.

3. Now see if you want more relief from the feeling. If you do, take 70 percent of that feeling and transfer it into the container, just as you did before, by counting from one to three.

4. Now in your imagination, send that container down into the molten core of the earth, where the feeling will be instantly transformed into energy that is useful and life-giving.

5. Be sure to keep some of all of your feelings, even the ones you don't like. We need to have some of all our feelings on hand to protect and defend ourselves and to provide information necessary for our best functioning.

Exercise 2: Release and Let Go

The purpose of this exercise is to allow you to release intense feelings in a way that is not harmful to you or others.

1. Pick a feeling or feelings that you want to release.

2. Start walking. As your feet hit the ground and as your arms reach the farthest arc in front of your body, say, "I am now going to release 70 percent of all the anger I feel right now. I am letting the anger travel down into the molten core of the earth every time my foot hits the ground. My anger is instantly transformed into energy that is useful and life-giving. I am letting the anger travel out the ends of my fingers, releasing the anger into the farthest reaches of the universe, where it will be instantly transformed into energy that is useful and life-giving."

3. Do this exercise for one to two minutes and then see how you are feeling. If you still need to release some feelings, repeat the exercise.

4. You can use this exercise for any feeling.

5. Never release all of any feeling. You need some of each feeling for your own protection and well-being.

As thinking beings, we often forget we are also animals, with the instincts and physiology of animals. As we move into adulthood, we forget the rhythm of our bodies. A child or dog wakes in the morning, stretches fully and completely, then walks, then drinks, then runs. Breathing deeply and fully, the young one automatically takes care of its physical self. It's a natural process. We adults are often out of touch with our most basic needs. We forget to stretch, breathe deeply, walk and run. These self-regulating techniques allow us to discover ways of reconnecting with our own vitality.

Soothing the Passionate Feelings

In order to calm the stormy internal landscape of passionate feelings, you must learn to reduce the intensity of your feelings so you can go forward with restored equilibrium. The following set of exercises helps reduce intense feelings, particularly anger, rage, envy, jealousy, and fear. Moving through the exercises helps you feel more calm and in touch with yourself. You will feel more alive and centered by reducing the intensity of your hyper-activated physiology.

Exercise 3: Giving Voice

1. Write down your angry feelings. Limit yourself to ten minutes using a kitchen timer if necessary. Let it rip. Don't worry about grammar or punctuation. This is not literature—this is dumping toxic waste—clearing it out of your body, brain, heart, mind, spirit, and also clearing the biochemistry of anger all the way out of your entire being, including each and every cell in your body.

2. Do not read what you have written. (It would only reinfect you.)

3. Get rid of the angry writing—rip it up, burn it. As you dispose of the angry writing, say to yourself, "I am sending this angry energy down into the molten core of the earth, where it will be instantly transformed into useful and life-giving energy."

That is, after all, what Mother Earth does all the time for us. Somehow, graciously, Mother Earth filters our waste and renews our energy. The smoggy air is diluted and transported by rain and snow and wind, filtered by the earth and the plants.

Exercise 4: Deep Muscle Relaxation

This exercise is designed to allow you to become more aware of your own states of tension and relaxation. Working with this exercise enables you to begin to control how tense or how relaxed you feel. After practicing a few times, you should experience a state of deeper relaxation. This exercise can be used both in emergencies and as an ongoing practice to connect you more deeply and completely with your ability to calm yourself. You can put this exercise onto an audiotape and let your own voice guide you to a state of even deeper calmness.

You are going to tense all the muscles in your body, group by group. Then you are going to relax all the large muscle groups, step by step.

Breathe naturally and fully as you move through the relaxation exercise. Let your breath move in and out in its own natural rhythm. You will find that by the end of the exercise, you will be breathing more deeply.

1. Raise your arms and squeeze your hands into fists. Hold the tension while you count to ten. Feel the strain, the tension. Now release the tension in your fists, remembering to say the word "relax" to yourself. Let all the tension go as you let your hands drop into your lap. Feel the wonderful warm relaxed feeling that comes from the absence of tension. Did you notice how much energy and effort it takes to remain tense, and did you notice that it takes absolutely no energy or effort to relax your muscles?

2. Hold your hands, palms together, in front of you as though praying, and push them against each other. Feel the tension; study the tension while you count to ten. Now relax. Let all the tension drain away and let yourself experience how good it feels to let all the tension go. Relax more.

3. Frown hard and tense the muscles of your forehead and the top of your head. Hold the tension while you count to ten. Notice and observe the tension. Now relax. Relax more. Let

all the tension go. Let yourself experience how good it feels to let all the tension go.

4. Wrinkle your nose. Squint your eyes. Feel the tension in the muscles around your eyes and across the top of your cheeks and upper lip. Hold the tension. Study the tension. Now relax. Let all the tension go. Let all the tension evaporate. Let yourself experience how good it feels to let all the tension go.

5. Draw the corners of your mouth back as if you were going to snarl. Observe the tension. Feel the tension. Hold the tension while you count to ten. Now relax. Let all the tension go. Let yourself experience how good it feels to let all the tension go.

6. Pull your chin down toward your chest and feel the tension in the back of your neck. Notice the tension while you count to ten. Feel the tension. Now let all the tension go. Let all the tension drain away. Relax more.

7. Take a deep breath while pulling your shoulders back and trying to make your shoulder blades touch. Observe the tension. Feel the tension while you count to ten. Now let all the tension go. Let all the tension drain away and let yourself experience how good it feels to let all the tension go.

8. Tighten up your stomach muscles. Notice the tension while you count to ten. Feel the tension. Now let all the tension go. Let all the tension drain away and let yourself experience how good it feels to let all the tension go.

9. Lift your legs slightly, just a little bit, and tighten the muscles in your thighs. Hold the tension while you count to ten. Observe the tension. Now let all the tension drain away. Let all the tension go. Relax more.

10. Tighten the muscles in your buttocks. Tighten. Tighten. Tighten. Feel the tension. Study the tension while you count to ten. Now let all the tension go. Let all the tension drain away and relax more.

11. Leaving your heels on the ground, point your toes up toward your head. Feel the tension in your calves while you count to ten. Now relax. Let all the tension go. Let all the tension drain away. Relax more.

12. Push down with your toes onto the floor. Feel the tension in your feet and ankle. Push down with your toes. Notice the

tension while you count to ten. Experience the tension. Now let all the tension go. Let all the tension drain away. Relax more.

Check where you are on the feeling intensity scale. If you are at a 5 or lower, go on to the next exercise. If you are above a 5 on the feeling intensity scale, repeat this exercise and then proceed to the next exercise.

Exercise 5: Slow Stretching

This exercise helps you reduce the intensity of passionate feelings. Moving through the exercise helps you feel more calm and more in touch with yourself. You can put this exercise on tape and listen to it

Imagine you are a big, lazy cat. After a night of hunting, racing, running, you are ready to prowl around your den, making sure everything is safe and secure. Everything is just exactly where it should be. One by one, you luxuriously stretch each leg to the very limit. Each leg, in turn, throbs in the deliciousness of the exaggerated full stretch. You turn your regal head slowly, completely stretching all the tendons and ligaments, breathing regularly and deeply. Your jaw drops down and your lips pull back, all the way back, as a huge, full yawn begins at the tips of your toes and unfolds throughout your whole body. You sink to the ground. It's warm and soothing. You snuffle and gently paw around in the earth to find just the right spot. You close your eyes and slowly drift away. Check in with your body. See what's going on. Notice any areas of your body where you feel tense and tight. Remember, you are a big cat. Let go into deep and satisfying relaxation. Breathe deeply and contentedly as you relax, even more deeply and completely.

Exercise 6: Walking to Serenity

This exercise is designed to help you feel more calm, cool, and collected. The purpose is to feel more alive and centered. This exercise is especially useful for cooling down from the passionate feelings of anger, rage, jealousy, fear, and envy.

Begin to imagine yourself walking. You may want to close your eyes. It's a beautiful day. The sun is shining, warming the back of your neck and shoulders. The air is fresh and clear. It smells slightly sweet. You hear the sound of birds softly chirping. You look at the beautiful, velvety green trees. You move along and finally hit your stride, arms swinging, feet setting down with purpose. The rhythm courses through you. You are in exactly the right place at the right time. You stride out. You begin to imagine walking and walking, on and on. It just feels right.

Just for the fun of it, start walking. Get up and walk wherever you are. Experience how good it feels to just use your body. Let your breathing take over and move up from the center of the earth into your body. Let yourself feel connected to yourself, to the earth. Breathe in and out as you move. It feels good.

Try walking outside. Look around. See the green and the gray and the blue. Open your nose and smell the freshness of being outside, the wonderful green smells. Pay attention to street noises, the cars, the barking dogs.

Try it. Five minutes of walking a day can change how you experience your life. Just walk for five minutes a day. See what happens.

If you are in a situation where you can't physically walk, imagine walking: the sounds, smells, the movement of your arms reaching out, your feet hitting the ground.

Exercise 7: Relaxed Breathing

This deep-breathing exercise assists you in doing what comes naturally to healthy dogs, cats, and children. By the time we have made it to adulthood, we have pretty much forgotten how to breathe deeply and fully. This exercise will help you breathe like you really mean it. Focus your attention on your breath. Begin to notice how you can get your breath to go deeper in your chest just by imagining the breath going deeper.

Don't worry about taking in more air—forget the idea of great gulps of air. Focus on the notion of your breath going deeper. You can begin to imagine your breath starting in your stomach. It's pretty amazing. Just let your breath start in your belly and go from there. Let your stomach muscles relax. Breathe down into your belly. You will notice your belly protrudes when you inhale, and contracts when you exhale.

Now as you continue breathing, imagine your breath starting in your buttocks. Let your breath begin in your pelvis and travel from there.

Now let your breath begin in your feet; your feet are flat on the ground, connected with the earth. Let your breath begin in your feet, and move from there.

Now, just for the fun of it, let your breath begin in your hands. Let your breath start its journey in your hands. If you are seated, it helps to place your hands in your lap or on the arms of your chair. See it. Imagine it. Let your breath begin in your hands and travel from there.

Now, let your breath begin at the very top of your head. Imagine opening your head, the top of your head, to the heavens. Let the breath gently pour into the top of your head from the very sky. It feels weird at first, and then you begin to get the rhythm of it. Let your breath gently begin from outside of you, from the sky above.

Let your breath come up from the earth below. What better than the sky above and the earth below to assist with the natural rhythm of your breathing?

Next step: Yoga Breathing. Try breathing using a traditional Yoga breathing technique.

Inhale, while you count: 1 . . . 2 . . . 3 . . . 4 . . .
Hold the breath, while you count: 1 . . . 2 . . . 3 . . . 4 . . .
Exhale, while you count: 1 . . . 2 . . . 3 . . . 4 . . . 5 . . . 6 . . .

Repeat this sequence several times until you begin to feel a rhythm in your breathing. Yoga breathing is particularly effective as a one-minute intervention to break up patterned responses to stress. It's short and easy to use. Try it four or five times a day and see what happens. You may want to put this exercise on audiotape to help you relax into the breathing. Play around with changing the count. Work with what best suits you.

Exercise 8: Rock-a-Bye Baby

It's no accident that babies calm down when they are rocked. The movement quiets an overwrought nervous system.

1. Rock in a rocking chair. Put on some soft music and gently rock.

2. Rock as you are sitting in an ordinary chair. Just move back and forth. Let your shoulders move slowly back and forth.

3. Get on your hands and knees on the floor and rock up, forward, and back, letting thighs and butt roll toward your calves. Play around with this. Do it slowly. Find the pace and

the posture that suits you. You will establish your own rhythm.

4. Now, imagine rocking. There are times and places where you can't physically rock. You can imagine rocking and that itself can be very soothing. Just imagine rocking, in detail—how it feels all over your body.

Exercise 9: Relax More

It is important to have a relaxation signal to help you calm down immediately. Practice this exercise regularly and you will discover that you are able to relax in a matter of seconds. Tie this relaxation signal to the relaxation response you already developed with deep muscle relaxation, deep breathing, or imagery.

Relaxation signals that are easy to use are visual signals and auditory signals. Some people are able to imagine a pattern in their mind's eye. It can be a circle or a square. It can be the corner of the room you are in. The simpler the better. Some people have difficulty imaging a pattern or a shape. They are often able to imagine a sooth-ing sound and can use it as a signal to calm themselves. See which approach works better for you.

- Imagine a circle, a square, or any shape that pleases you. Imagine the shape outlined in black on a white background. See the shape in sharp detail. Now, see the shape outlined in white on a black background. Let yourself really see the sharply defined outline. Visualize it clearly. This shape will be your immediate signal to relax and calm yourself. The more you use it, the more effective it will be.

- Imagine a sound that pleases you. For example, imagine the sound of water running in a brook: the fresh splashing and gurgling, bubbling drip and drop of water. You can even turn on the tap for a minute and listen to the sound of the water splashing into the basin or tub. Use the sound signal to relax quickly in the moment. The more you use it, the better it will work.

- Feel the sensation as you press gently into your palm with the thumb of your other hand. Use this as an immediate sig-nal to relax. The slight sensation of pressure will be your sig-nal to relax and calm yourself.

Activating the Softer Feelings

The following group of exercises will assist you when you are feeling sad, vulnerable, hurt, confused, depressed, overwhelmed, helpless. These techniques help you with these less volatile but still painful and very essential feelings.

Exercise 10: Talking to Yourself

The ongoing conversation you have with yourself is the longest conversation in your entire life. Talking to yourself when you feel upset can be very helpful.

You might say:

- "How I feel now isn't going to last forever. I feel horrible. I have felt horrible before and I lived through it. I can remember that I have been here before and come out the other side." Remember specific situations that have been horribly stressful. Remember how you worked things out and felt better.

- "I have seen other people get through this. I know other people have gotten through feeling awful—I've seen it. Somehow they go on. I have done it before. Even though this is different, I know I can do it again."

- "I may feel bad, but I know I am not a bad person. I can't let anybody put me down. I have to let myself know and really feel and believe that I am loved by others. I am going to love myself."

Create your own unique dialogue for your specific situation. Talk kindly and gently to yourself, reassuring yourself of your essential goodness and strength. You may initially have to imagine that you are doing this for another person. This is another exercise that works well on audiotape.

Exercise 11: Giving Thanks

Use this exercise when you are feeling sorry for yourself, when you feel depleted and deflated.

Make a list (it helps to write it down) of all the things you have to be grateful for. This may include such things as:

- I am alive.

- I can move and talk and breathe. I can eat. I have food and shelter.

- I have choices about many things in my life.

Make an ongoing list of the specific things you can be grateful for. Add to it. Add one thing a day. The list can go on and on. Read it one time every day.

Being human, we tend to focus on our flaws, on the things we don't have. Make the "thanks" list and see what happens. Your assessment of who and what you are will get more in balance; so will your self-esteem.

Exercise 12: A Time and a Place for Me

Life presses in on all of us. We face demands and needs from ourselves, our jobs, our loved ones. Use this exercise as a refuge, as a way to center and rebalance yourself.

Begin to allow yourself to remember or create a beautiful place for yourself. Your special place can be real or imaginary. For example, your special place might be outside, sitting nestled in a warm rock by the banks of a gorgeous, rushing stream. You listen to the gently gurgling water and take in the fresh wild scents that surround you. The sound of the stream comforts you. Water bubbles over rocks. You gaze into a light, creamy blue sky. Soft white clouds float gently across the horizon.

You begin to notice the deep warmth of the sun-baked rock on your back. It cuddles you close. The deep heat slowly penetrates your back, your legs, your arms. You sink gently and slowly further into the rock, letting the glow enfold you. You feel at home, safe, complete, at peace with everything. You let yourself enjoy the absolute feeling of contentment. Your world is timeless and complete.

Know that you can return to your special place whenever you want. It's right there waiting for you. All you have to do is open a little space in your mind's eye. Your special place can be inside or outside. Enjoy.

Exercise 13: Giving to Yourself

The purpose of this exercise is to offer to yourself what you often give to others, almost without thinking. This exercise provides you with the encouragement and affirmation you need to get through tough times. Here are some suggestions of things you can do for yourself:

- Leave a message for yourself on your answering machine. Make it really kind. This takes a little bit of practice because it often seems easier to be kind to someone else. For example, you might say: "I know you have been having a rough time and that you're feeling discouraged. It's going to get better. You have been doing a really good job in a tough situation. I am proud of you for hanging in there. I love you."

- Make a date with yourself to do something fun, just like you would make a date with a friend. Create a specific time for the date with yourself in your schedule. Do something enjoyable. Go on a walk. Get a cup of coffee at a place you really like. See a movie. Go to the park and swing on the swings.

- Go to the store and find a card to send to yourself. You are in the best position of anyone in the world to pick out the absolutely right card for you. It can be funny, sweet, saucy, whatever you want. Write a tender, loving message to yourself. Sign it with love.

Make up more things to do for yourself that will specifically please you and give you what you need for the tough spot you're going through at a particular moment.

Exercise 14: Keep On Dancin'

This exercise assists you in getting yourself going when the going is tough. If you're feeling immobilized by depression, try dancing. It will get your blood flowing, make you feel more alive and better about yourself.

Turn on some music that turns you on. Get up and move around the room. Be expansive. Let it rip. Feel the beat. Let the music move through you. Flap your arms like a bird. Move your head like a turkey. Lumber, heavy footed, like an elephant. Let the music move you.

You can also dance in your imagination. Let the tension flow out of your hands and feet as you imagine dancing, slowly and languorously, fast and furious. Let the music move you and move through you, even as you sit. Imagine.

Exercise 15: Out With the Old

Soaking in a tub is just plain good self-care, with the added benefit of letting all the accumulated yuck of the day run down the drain. It is particularly helpful on days when you have had to cope with conflict, stress, and too many demands.

Take one cup of apple cider vinegar or one cup of Epsom salts or sea salt and put it in your bath. As you prepare the bath, let yourself imagine that all your accumulated physical and psychological stress and tension will wash away. Let yourself imagine that all your stress and tension can go into the bathwater and be transformed into life-giving water that will return to the earth and be useful.

Soak for a while. When you're ready, get out of the tub and rinse in the shower. Allow the icky stuff you have absorbed in the wear and tear of your daily life to go right down the drain. Experience your own deep cleansing as the tub is emptied of yuck. See what happens with this cleansing ritual. It's pretty amazing.

Exercise 16: Reading for Pleasure

This exercise is designed to provide you with an experience in giving yourself pleasure. You deserve it. Providing yourself pleasure over time improves your self-esteem. Providing pleasure to yourself is a meta-message, from you to you, that you are worthwhile and deserving.

Read something you love, a junk novel, a mystery, biography, the *Wall Street Journal*, just for fifteen or twenty minutes. If you are really willing to luxuriate, take forty minutes or an hour to sink into your book or magazine. Bask in the pleasure of reading for fun, for enjoyment, for pleasure. Give yourself simple moments of pleasure. Even five minutes a day of uninterrupted pleasure can make a big difference in how you feel about yourself and your life.

Exercise 17: Getting a Perspective

After using some of the previous techniques to get yourself to a 2 or 3 on the 0–10 feeling intensity scale you are ready and able to use your thinking skills to help yourself feel even better, more soothed.

Find out where the crunch is, where the agitated, anxious feelings are coming from. Scan your particular situation and see if you have work pressure, conflict at home, loneliness.

Sometimes we are able to locate the reasons for why we feel lousy. Sometimes it helps just to know why. Other times the feelings are more free-floating, less attached to a specific event. At these times of free-floating bad feelings, we often feel the residue of an old, difficult experience which has moved forward from the past and enveloped us. You can look at these free-floating bad feelings as things you've lost, that are in the process of being found and metabolized into something useful, perhaps a deeper understanding of your past. You're getting perspective.

It's all part of your experience. Your capacity to feel good is directly related to your capacity to feel all your feelings, the good, the bad, and the ugly. If you can't find where the feelings come from, keep looking. It helps. If at times you can't find a reason for your malaise, you should just accept that you are processing old painful feelings and that you will come through it. Use self-soothing techniques to provide respite and relief from the intrusion of past and present painful feelings.

Regaining Emotional Balance

Take some time to practice the exercises in this chapter. Try each exercise and see how it feels. Get to know what each exercise does for your body and your state of mind. If you practice, you will know how to use them when you need them. As with all things in life, you have to be prepared in order to succeed. If you suddenly find yourself at a 7 or 8 on the feeling intensity scale, you can do an exercise, but it will bring more relief if you've already practiced it. If you practice tensing your muscles and letting them relax, and if you practice deep breathing, you will be better prepared for the moment when you need to relax. You will be able to restore emotional balance at those times when you need it most. Five minutes a day will create improvement.

By learning to restore yourself, you will feel better and better over time. You will be able to go into stressful situations knowing that you have powerful techniques to help you regain emotional balance. Every bit of self-care sends a message to your body that everything is going to be okay. The self-soothing and self-activating exercises will help you restore emotional balance. You will be on your way to establishing healthy self-esteem.

CHAPTER 6

Facing the Mirror
On the Wall

In order to have healthy total self-esteem, you need to have a realistic view of yourself: wonderful in some ways, average in others, flawed and limited in others. To have the most resilient self-esteem, you need to be able to see yourself as you really are, without judging yourself. Knowing who you really are allows you to take credit for your strengths and make a decision to change something you don't like about yourself. You need to be able to look in the mirror and have the mirror reflect back the truth.

Self-objectivity is the ability to accurately assess strengths and weaknesses in yourself.

First, in order to be objective about yourself, you need to understand that temperamental factors, such as attention-deficit disorder, learning disorders, a familial tendency to gain weight, or a predisposition to anxiety or depression, are biologically driven and not anyone's fault. If you don't recognize the origin of such characteristics, you may feel unnecessarily ashamed or defective. The more you are anchored in understanding your own history—who you really are and why you are that way—the less vulnerable you will be to making destructive assumptions about who you are and how you became the way you are.

Your total self-esteem is made up of your perceptions about yourself and the value you place on each self-perception. As discussed in chapter 1, you may perceive yourself in a number of ways. Along with perceptions of yourself, you automatically include explicit or implicit value judgments about these attributes.

Total self-esteem includes both your perceptions of, and feelings about, qualities and characteristics of yourself in several arenas: your physical self; your emotional, intellectual, and spiritual selves; and yourself in relation to others.

Characteristics of Realistic Self-Esteem

Realistic self-esteem is characterized by a strong convergence between your description of yourself and how others perceive you. It is true that others may perceive aspects of you that are out of your awareness. Also, there are aspects of you that are private and unobservable. Nonetheless, a significant overlap between your view and others' views of you is an essential ingredient of realistic self-esteem.

Realistic self-esteem includes positives and negatives. Almost everyone has both positive and negative qualities, and positive and negative behavior. Your self-esteem is not realistic if you see yourself as all good or all bad.

You should also be able to describe yourself in a detailed way, including your specific strengths and weaknesses.

Another way to determine if you have realistic self-esteem is by how frequently you receive feedback from others about what they like and don't like about you. If you receive little or no feedback from others (bosses, co-workers, family members, friends), it may be that others perceive you as too fragile to tolerate feedback. It may be that you repel constructive criticism. Either scenario is a good indicator that you do not have realistic self-esteem.

Unrealistic Self-Esteem

Unrealistic self-esteem occurs when there is a gap between your view of yourself and others' perceptions of you. The greater the disparity between how you perceive yourself and how others perceive you, the more likely it is that you possess unrealistic self-esteem.

Most of us suffer from low self-esteem, never quite measuring up to our own expectations. A smaller group of us cause others to suffer from our inflated self-esteem (nobody else ever measures up to our expectations).

Understanding Your Low Self-Esteem

The process of unraveling the mystery of your low self-esteem is both scary and exciting, as mysteries often are. Understanding what really happened in the past is frightening for several reasons. In seeing what really happened, you must accept that your parents were less than perfect, that they were human and flawed in some way. That means that you have to give up the dream that your childhood was perfect, your parents were perfect, and that if you had just done something differently, had been better, you would have gotten all your needs met.

It is frightening to give up the dream of a perfect childhood. If you give up this fantasy, you must accept that the things you did not get in childhood (unconditional love and acceptance) are things you will never to be able to get in the way you wanted and needed as a child. To give up the dream of the perfect childhood means that you must give up the quest for the perfect mate, the perfect children, the perfect job, the perfect self.

On the positive side, giving up the dream enables you to create healthy self-esteem. Giving up the dream of the perfect mate allows you to possibly find a real mate with whom you can create a real relationship. Giving up the dream of perfect children allows you to see and enjoy the uniqueness of your own children. Giving up the dream of the perfect self allows you to find out who you really are, recognizing and creating a more spontaneous, real self.

Characteristics of Unrealistic Low Self-Esteem

Devaluation of yourself.

This takes the form of: "I'm bad, no good, incompetent. I don't really know how to be good at anything. I'm going to be found out and then humiliated." Or, "No one really likes me; no one really knows me. If people knew me, they wouldn't like me." Or, "I'm too, fat (or skinny, old, young, quiet, loud, tall, short, black, white, feminine, masculine, aggressive, passive, rigid), so I'll never be loved or accepted." Or, "I'm not attractive (beautiful, thin, witty, old, young, smart, dumb, rich), so I will never be loved for who I am."

If you say things like this to yourself, you're devaluing who you are.

Inability to identify, acknowledge, and take pride in your good qualities and accomplishments.

You may realize that you don't acknowledge your good qualities. Does the following statement sound familiar to you?

"I often point out, to myself and others, that I could do better. If I walk for fifteen minutes, I notice that I say, 'I could have done more. I should be running five miles, not walking fifteen minutes. Other people do far more exercise. I only walked once this week.'" If this sounds like you, you're not taking pride in your accomplishments.

Difficulty in accepting a compliment and basking in the good feeling. Does the following sound like you?

"When someone gives me a compliment, I feel kind of uneasy. I find myself saying, 'I only paid ten dollars for it. It's really old. Your outfit looks better. My husband hates this outfit.'"

Overvaluing others.

You see yourself as significantly less than you really are. Low self-esteem can make you timid, afraid to take risks, stodgy, boring, and dull, especially to yourself. Low self-esteem can prevent you from exploring your creativity and your potential: as an artist, as an athlete, as a spiritual being, as a person in relationships with others, giving, taking, learning, growing. Low self-esteem can make you apologetic about excellent work you've done and only lukewarm about resounding success.

Low self-esteem can diminish joy, exultation, and pride in your body; it can bury sexual and sensual pleasure.

Sandy's Story

On the surface, Sandy seems to have it all. She has risen rapidly in her company to her position as a managing partner. Her subordinates envy her looks, her money, and her poise under fire. She is extremely competent and liked by nearly everyone. She dresses with flair and dates a lot.

When she is "on" for the public, Sandy seems confident, outgoing, and appears to be loaded with self-esteem, but in her private life, Sandy is angry and unhappy much of the time. She drinks too much and she is unable to form a lasting relationship with a man. Her friends are concerned, afraid she is headed for disaster. She takes criticism so badly, they are afraid to tell her how worried they are about her.

Sandy's problem is that deep down inside, she doesn't think much of herself. Though others see a lovely face, when the shining star of the company looks in the mirror she dissects every flaw—the nose off center, the waist too high, cellulite on her thighs. She repeatedly replays interaction and conversation with others, agonizing over what she should have said or done to make a better impression. Her greatest fear is that people will find out she's a fraud—that she's not really as talented or congenial as they think she is—and that her career will soon be in shambles. Focusing on her private life fills her with hopelessness, so she puts more energy into work than she knows she should.

Many of us may not be as outwardly successful as Sandy, but many of us share, in varying degrees, unhealthy attitudes about our self-worth.

Sandy illustrates the most common self-esteem problem for women, low self-esteem. Sandy's low self-esteem is camouflaged by how good she looks on the outside. Constantly finding and feeling her flaws, nothing she does enables her to feel quite good enough about herself. Sandy finds it difficult to recognize and claim her positive qualities and attributes. She is her own worst enemy. Something important feels like it's missing inside, in spite of her considerable achievements.

Low self-esteem is often related to overuse of drugs and alcohol, depression, anxiety, problems with weight, overworking, underachieving, emptiness, loneliness, and poor relationships.

Inflated Self-Esteem

Some women have the opposite problem: undervaluing others. Inflated self-esteem is another form of unrealistic self-esteem.

Inflated self-esteem is the inability to acknowledge the faults, flaws, and imperfections we all have. People with inflated self-esteem make others feel bad in big and little ways; any problem is someone else's fault. Inflated self-esteem hides a deep sense of impoverishment typically associated with a lot of denial. "I lost my job because the boss was envious of my creativity—he couldn't stand the competition." "My husband can't stand nagging because he is too thin-skinned." "I flunked the test because the teacher has it in for me."

Naomi's Story

Naomi, unlike Sandy, seems criticism-proof. Whatever anyone else has experienced or achieved, Naomi has felt more or accomplished more. She offers her experience and wisdom to others, even when they don't want it. Gossip and criticism of others are the mainstays of her conversation. She finds flaws in everyone's situation and personality. Naomi is a teacher and intellectually brilliant, so she draws students to her, but there is no real intimacy in her life. Her self-absorption and sharp tongue drive people away from her.

Both Sandy and Naomi are unable to assess themselves realistically. Sandy explains away or minimizes her positive attributes, never taking credit for her multitude of strengths. Sandy's feelings and thoughts about herself are sometimes denigrating and awful—a constant litany of imagined failures and mistakes—she is never quite good enough. Naomi, on the other hand, sees others as flawed, almost subhuman, never quite up to her standards. She sees herself as larger than life, her way is *the* way, whether it is making coffee or giving advice. Neither Sandy with low self-esteem, nor Naomi, with inflated self-esteem, is realistic about who she is.

Difficulties with figuring out your strengths and weaknesses result in your being too hard on yourself, or too hard on others, or some mix of the two styles. This places limits on your creativity, accomplishments, relatedness, and liveliness. Your ability to see yourself as you really are—blemished in some ways, beautiful and unique in others, ordinary in some ways—allows you to acknowledge, build on, and maximize your strengths, take credit for your adequacies, and decide which qualities you might want to improve

Claudia's Story: An Example of Realistic Self-Esteem

Claudia is like the old woman in the shoe. She has so many friends she almost doesn't know what to do. Forty-six and childless, Claudia quit her job, living a trimmed down life to become the writer she always knew she was.

Claudia is smart, warm, intellectual, a closet extrovert in an overweight body. She is able to connect in a way that allows another person to feel truly seen and heard. Friends adore her responsiveness and spontaneous directness. Claudia's exquisite sensitivity to others, acceptance of her limitations, and her ability to acknowledge her own deep resources endears her to others. Her life is rich.

Characteristics of Self-Objectivity

Being able to see yourself for who you are is essential to healthy self-esteem. If you're like Claudia, you are able to accept and appreciate yourself; you're also able to recognize others for who they are.

When you have self-objectivity and good total self-esteem, you are able to find creative solutions to the problems and disappointments inevitable in life, moving through crises by achieving small and significant increments of mastery. You are not perfect: you struggle with anxiety and sadness and depression like everyone else, but you have the ability to nourish yourself, and to know, when the going gets tough, that your well of sufficient selfhood will return. You are able to give freely and able to ask for and accept help graciously. If you have strong self-objectivity and good total self-esteem you believe that your life, although sometimes stormy and difficult, will continue to become richer and better

The Sky's the Limit

It is absolutely possible for you to learn the skills for self-objectivity and healthier self-esteem, even if you carry a lot of bad feelings about yourself from your past. The process of creating your own healthier self-esteem began when you started reading this book. Your effort and investment in yourself in buying this book is a message to you, from you, that you are deserving and worthy of healthy self-esteem.

Your internal resources, those you know about and those hidden from your view, are a source of enormous power on your journey to healthy self-esteem. As you continue reading, you will find that you have more self-esteem resources than you are already acknowledge. In fact, you have many more.

Exercise: Assessing Your Self-Esteem

The purpose of this exercise is to help you identify areas of your functioning that reflect low self-esteem, inflated self-esteem, and healthy total self-esteem.

You may have some areas of inflated self-esteem. ("I'm a better writer than most of those that get published. Getting published is who you know, and I don't know anyone influential, so there's no point in even submitting a manuscript.")

You may have areas of low self-esteem. ("Even though my doctor and my husband and my girlfriends tell me I'm not overweight and that I look great, I don't believe them. I think I should lose fifteen pounds.")

You do have some areas of healthy realistic self-esteem, but they may not be easy for you to identify. You may help others, give compliments, be supportive and nurturing when someone is struggling, and offer compassion, empathy, and kindness. These are all self-esteem strengths, and you need to claim them. If you give too much to others, you can still take credit for acts of caring, and note that you carry it too far and need to monitor and perhaps modify how much you give.

The following sets of questions will help you identify areas of weakness and strength in your self-esteem.

Questions for Unrealistic Low Self-Esteem

- Are you consistently finding flaws in yourself?

- Do you expect yourself to be perfect most of the time and get mad at yourself when you are not?

- Do you have hateful feelings toward your body or other aspects of yourself?

- Do you often feel worthless, ashamed, or bad?

- Do you find it difficult to know what your feel?

- Do you frequently sacrifice healthy self-care to take care of others?

- Do you find yourself living mostly in the past or the future?

Questions for Unrealistic Inflated Self-Esteem

- Do those close to you tell you that you are selfish? Self-absorbed? Unable to listen? Abusive?

- Do you frequently blame or criticize others?

- Do you secretly believe yourself to be superior to others?

- Do you tend to lose control when you don't get your own way?

- Do you find yourself frequently disappointed and angry with other people?

- Do others give you constructive criticism or negative feedback on a regular basis?

Questions for Realistic Self-Esteem

- Can you write a detailed list of your strengths and weaknesses?

- Do you know what you feel most of the time?

- Are you able to reduce the intensity of your feelings when you want to?

- Are you able to get yourself going when you are depressed?

- Are you happy to be alive?

- Are you able to recover your zest for life when you are knocked off balance by crisis or loss?

- Do you enjoy other people and see their strengths as well as their weaknesses?

- Are you able to identify the specific shortcomings of others, along with acknowledging their good qualities?

- Do you get over your mistakes quickly, without punishing yourself emotionally?

- Do you find real pleasure in your daily life?

- Do you have fun at least once a day?

- Are you proud of your body?

- Do you take good care of your body?

- Are you able to accept compliments?

- Are you able to acknowledge and evaluate criticism?

Use your answers to these questions to help you evaluate your self-esteem.

You can come back to these questions a few weeks from now, after working on improving your self-esteem, to see how your answers have changed.

Exercise: Assessing Your Self-Objectivity

The purpose of this exercise is to help you figure out your particular strengths and weaknesses in self-objectivity, your ability to see yourself as you really are. This exercise will help you find the truth about how you are functioning in the different areas of your life. When you have completed this exercise, you will be able to take more credit for the strengths that surface and you will be able to see if there is something you want to change about yourself.

Describe how you feel about yourself under the categories that follow, using the examples as a springboard. Then go back and reevaluate each area of your functioning as though it were being rated by your kindest and most truthful friend.

Accepting Your Body When You Really Hate It

Body-type and body-image example:

"I have some difficulty accepting my body type—it just isn't what I would like it to be. I have these wide hips and big thighs, and no matter what I do with exercise or diet, I can't make a change. My body image isn't very good. I compare myself to how I think I'm supposed to look and I don't have the totally toned slim body I would like. I feel stuck."

Body-talk example:

"If I'm honest, I have to admit that I sometimes say mean things about my body. I do say things to myself about my body that I wouldn't say to a friend about her body. I can be kind to myself about a lot of things, but accepting my body isn't one of them. I do get angry at my body because it won't change in the ways that I want it to. I sometimes hate parts of my body because I think they're ugly and gross. Like the dimpled cellulite on my thighs. Ugh!"

Body feedback example:

"Thank heaven I finally got to an area of my body where I function pretty well. I am able to tune into what my body is telling me most of the time. I can tell when I'm on the verge of a cold and can slow myself down and take extra vitamins and baby myself. I injured my knee running ten years ago and I notice every little thing about that knee, and I know how to respond to problems with my knee by increasing strengthening exercises and backing off aerobics."

Nutrition example:

"My nutrition is good in general. I do notice that I start cramming junk food when I am dealing with a lot of stress, but I don't seem to be able to notice it in time to do anything to stop it. Once in a while I get into a pattern of stuffing at night while I'm watching TV. I don't know what this is about."

Physical exercise example:

"Relief is washing over me. Another area where I do pretty well. I used to be a long distance runner and I absolutely loved the high and the discipline. Since my daughter was born, I've had to give up putting in those daily miles. I have to give myself credit here because I was able to make the shift into being more flexible about what I do for exercise. Now, I might do some power walking on my lunch hour. I've gotten some good exercise videos, so I sometimes do those. If nothing else, I will do twenty minutes of slow stretching, when I haven't exercised in a few days and can't find the time for anything else. I go through periods where it's hard to fit exercise in, but I do get back to it. I guess I get some points on this one."

Pleasure example:

"Okay, I guess this area is kind of a problem for me. I want to have more pleasure in my life, more fun, but it just seems hard to fit it in. I know that I support my daughter and my husband in receiving pleasure, like my daughter's dance lessons and my husband getting out to play golf, but it's definitely harder to do this for myself. I also notice that I'm not too interested in sex right now, or even that interested in cuddling. Everything else in my life is going pretty well, and it seems like I almost can't let myself have it all. I think this might be the area for me to focus on and change."

Rest example:

"This is another area where I have my good days and my bad days or weeks. Sometimes, I get into the rhythm of getting enough rest, and I feel good. I wake up in the morning and look forward to the day. I actually feel kind of excited about what might happen that could be fun or interesting. It's seems kind of mysterious and intriguing. In those days or weeks when I don't get enough rest, I get kind of cranky. Not really nasty, but I just don't have my same resilience. I guess I need to pay attention to this because I notice that I will shortchange myself on rest in order to do something for my husband or daughter, or even for the house."

Appearance example:

"I think I'm kind of variable on this. Some days I really make an effort, and I have to admit that I feel better when I look good. I mean, I'm not Michelle Pfieffer, but I can put myself together if I take the time. Other days, probably when I'm kind of discouraged or depressed, I just don't make the effort. I could, but I don't."

Time-for-myself example:

My report card on this one is mixed. Sometimes I can really hold the line, and I can tell my family that I have to have time for myself. Other days, I think it's mostly when I'm tired or depleted, I just don't seem to have the stuff to say 'No.' Those are the times when I cave in. I sometimes feel resentful later about doing that."

Healthy Selfishness

Example:

"I do feel deserving of good things in all areas of my life, and I can find only two areas of healthy selfishness that I could really improve. I know I have the ability to do a lot more professionally. I think sometimes I give too much credit to everyone else and don't claim what I contributed. This is probably holding me back in my job. The other thing is I notice that I do start feeling a little uneasy when my life is going really well in all areas. It seems like something bad might happen if I feel too good for too long. Like someone else might get jealous or envious."

Acquiring the Courage to Feel

Example:

"This is an area where I do really well, except for one kind of feeling. I notice that it is difficult for me to stop following the feminine script about anger and being nice. Sometimes I think that the service manager where I take my car is kind of talking down to me—almost contemptuously. I find myself being overly nice when he does this. I'd really like to say, 'Cut the kindergarten explanation and talk to me like I have a brain. I took auto shop in high school. I'm no dummy when it comes to cars.' I feel that I should say this, but I've never gotten up the courage."

Getting Off the Emotional Tightrope

Example:

"I do really well with getting myself out of a slump when I'm depressed or discouraged. I have a harder time in some situations, getting myself lower on the feeling intensity scale. A lot of those situations are ones where somebody is getting treated unfairly. I can escalate up to a 6 on the scale, and then I lose my ability to think clearly and present my best logical arguments about why the situation needs to change. I'd like to work on this area because I want to be more effective."

Rocketing Your Way to Self-Advocacy

Example:

"I am able to advocate well for other people. I have lots of courage and skills to do that. It is harder for me to advocate for myself. I sometimes wait too long in the doctor's office if it's for me. If it's for my daughter or my mother, that's another story. Watch out! In my job, I sometimes have difficulty telling my boss when I need extra help. I'll just stay late to get the project out on time. Also, when I get those creepy sales calls about changing telephone service or a time share in Mexico—sometimes it's just really hard for me to cut the other person off. After all, I'm supposed to be polite and nice. I definitely should take lessons from my husband on this one. He can get the most persistent salesperson off the phone in under one minute, and it doesn't bother him at all."

Working on People Skills, not People-Pleasing

Example:

"I think I'm pretty good at being assertive a lot of the time. I'm really good at communicating what I want and need with the employees I supervise. I know I do it in the right way, because I get lots of feedback about my great management style. The areas that are tougher are with my boss, and people who are really pushy. I kind of freeze in the moment with people who are superaggressive."

Becoming the Parent You Always Wanted

Example:

"I know I have some strengths here, but I could do better about giving myself more nurturing. The family I grew up in had lots of love, but it didn't come out in affection or saying 'I love you.' So that is probably a missing link for me. I probably don't baby myself enough and I think sometimes I don't expect enough for and of myself—like moving toward the big promotion I know I deserve."

After you've described how you feel about yourself in each of the above areas, be sure to reevaluate each area of your functioning as if you were a kind and truthful friend. You might also want to ask a close friend how she sees you functioning in the above areas. You might want to ask an exercise buddy, your husband, or a couple of co-workers about how they see you in the areas of your life they are familiar with. Compare the results you obtained from the composite information from your kind truthful friend with the initial assessment you did.

After completing this exercise, you should have a more realistic idea about where you want to work on your self-esteem.

CHAPTER 7

Rocketing Your Way to Self-Advocacy

External achievements and rewards by themselves do not build core self-esteem. Core self-esteem is developed in infancy and early childhood, and is then mediated by subsequent events and your response to them. But you can affect your core self-esteem as an adult by making a plan to move into action and become your own best advocate. An *advocate* is a friend or associate who supports, defends, justifies, advises, commends, and urges you to go forward and do your best. You may not have had the advocate you wanted or needed as an infant, child, or adult. Now is the time to create advocacy for yourself. *Self-advocacy* is the ability to consistently take action to improve your situation.

How Moving Into Action Improves Your Self-Esteem

Your core self-esteem can be influenced positively by your consistent use of self-esteem building techniques. Any self-esteem building technique when done with some consistency will provide improvement in your self-esteem. If you exercise, you will probably feel good about making the effort, your mood may improve, you will probably look better to yourself and you will enjoy the health benefits that come with exercising: improved circulation, better cardiovascular function, improved metabolism, increased bone density. These changes will have a positive impact on how you perceive yourself and how you feel about yourself, and will also change how others perceive you and feel about you.

In addition to these gains, when you do one self-esteem building technique with some regularity, you are delivering yourself a critically important psychological message: "I am good enough and worthwhile enough that I deserve the time and energy I devote to enhancing my self-esteem." It is this powerful meta-message that, over a period of time, will change your core self-esteem. Using self-esteem techniques themselves will produce some improvement in your self-esteem. Consistent *practice* of the techniques and taking credit for your efforts can produce positive changes in your deepest core self-esteem.

Giving Yourself Credit

To improve your self-esteem as quickly and effectively as possible, you must learn to take credit for all efforts you make, no matter how small or seemingly insignificant. Taking credit for achievements is difficult for many women. We don't want to brag. We frequently feel that unless we are perfect, we don't really deserve any credit. We sometimes think that our small achievements in daily life are not really worth much. We often find flaws in ourselves and what we are able to achieve. We often focus on the mistakes we make rather than on the positive results of what we do.

At first glance, pointing out how you could improve would seem the best way to motivate yourself. However, pointing out the flaws in your functioning without acknowledging your achievements is damaging to your self-esteem. Most of us can't grow and stretch and build better self-esteem when surrounded by negative feedback—especially if it is our own. In nurturing ourselves, we sometimes make the mistake of believing that the stick is more effective than the carrot. Nothing could be further from the truth. The most effective parents, bosses, teachers, and therapists work with the existing strengths in a person. In order to be your own best advocate, you need to create an atmosphere of respectful acknowledgment of your own progress, no matter how insignificant you believe it is.

How to Become Your Own Best Advocate

In order to become your own best advocate you need to:

1. *Clearly assess your current functioning* in all the important areas of your life—your physical health and well-being, your emotional well-being, your relationships, your finances, your spirituality.

2. *Clearly define your current expectations* in all the important areas of your life. Your expectations—what you foresee for yourself and what you believe is possible for you—define what you will achieve.

3. *Upgrade your expectations* for yourself. Your upgraded expectations will be the goals toward which you move. These higher expectations will define the action plan you create to propel you into your new goals.

Why Your Expectations for Yourself Are Critical to What Happens in Your Life

Expectations are what you believe about what is going to happen to you. Expectations are your desires, wishes, hopes, dreams, fantasies, both those you are aware of and the ones that are unconscious, that determine how things will be for you. What you expect determines which goals you will meet and exactly what you make of your life. Expectations shape how you will construct your reality—your self-esteem, your relationships, your emotional and physical health, your spirituality. Your expectations influence how rich or how poor you are in all areas of your functioning.

By upgrading your expectations you can greatly influence your immediate environment and your larger world. "This conscious change is brought about by the two qualities inherent in consciousness: attention and intention. Attention energizes, and intention transforms. Whatever you put your attention on will grow stronger in your life. Whatever you take your attention away from will wither, disintegrate, and disappear. Intention, on the other hand, triggers transformation of energy and information. Intention organizes its own fulfillment" (Chopra 1994, 70).

A client once confessed in therapy that her goal in life was to marry a millionaire, so that all her material wants and needs would be amply provided for. Her therapist wisely suggested that she upgrade and become a millionaire herself.

Exercise: How to Assess Your Current Functioning

The purpose of this exercise is to help you identify how you are functioning in your life and allow you to become familiar with the exact expectations you have for yourself. This exercise allows you to put Dr. Chopra's concept of attention to work for yourself. After completing it, you will know exactly where to focus your attention. Then you can decide what is good enough to leave alone and what you want to change.

In this exercise, you will look at each area of your life, observing how you function and what your current expectations are. Read the following example of how another woman, named Tina, completed the exercise, and then do the exercise yourself.

Tina's Functioning and Expectations

- **Tina's body functioning**: "I've had some problems with my immune system. I seem to get more than my share of colds and flu. I exercise very sporadically and I feel bad about that because I know how important it is. I just can't seem to do it. Nobody encouraged me to exercise when I was growing up, so I never got the habit of exercising. I feel okay about my body sometimes, but I notice that I am mean to myself if I gain weight."

- **Tina's body expectations**: "I know I need to be totally honest, or this won't do me any good. Things have been like they are for a long time, and I think everything will go on as it is. Sometimes I wish I were more active and could feel proud of walking or going to aerobics, but I think I'm lazy. I guess if I really think about it, my body will get worse if I don't do something to change my exercise."

- **Tina's emotional functioning**: "I think I know what I feel most of the time. I do a pretty good job of calming myself down when I'm upset. It's hard to get myself moving when I feel depressed. I wish I felt more joy and excitement. I think most of my relationships are good. I would like to be closer to my husband. It just seems like so much work."

- **Tina's emotional expectations**: "When I really look at it, I set pretty low goals for what I expect from my husband. I want us to be closer, but if I am honest, I am not convinced that we can figure out how to do that. I'm also kind of selfish because I don't know how much energy I want to put into the marriage. I have little time for myself as it is."

- **Tina's financial functioning**: "I do all right financially, there's always food on the table and a roof over our head. I'm not a risk taker, and sometimes I wish I had more of that quality. I've always had an interest in starting my own business, but I've been afraid to do it. I am artistic and I have a girlfriend who started her own handmade jewelry business part-time years ago, and she has fifteen employees. I can't imagine what it would be like to have a lot less worry about money."

- **Tina's financial expectations**: "I think I have kind of medium level expectations of what I can have financially. I think it goes with the 'little woman' syndrome—don't brag, don't show off, don't look foolish, don't be too loud, don't take the biggest piece of cake.'"

- **Tina's spiritual functioning**: "I have a lot of doubts about how I think and feel about the issue of spirituality. I am not religious, although I had to go to church as a kid, but I don't really feel settled on this issue. I don't know what happens after death, if anything happens. I do see some of my friends who seem to be in better shape on this issue. Whatever they think and feel about spirituality, they have a level of comfort with it that I don't."

- **Tina's spiritual expectations**: "I guess I'll just muddle along until I get too uncomfortable about this issue. I noticed that when my mom got sick a couple of years ago I really became concerned about what I believe."

Tina's Upgrade

Tina attended a class to improve her self-esteem. The instructor had the students complete the assessment about current life functioning and expectations that appears above.

Tina decided to upgrade her body expectations and created an action plan to achieve her new goals.

Your Upgrade

After you complete an assessment of your current life functioning and expectations, you can move onto the next step. Get some paper and write "My World Class Expectations" at the top of the page. Go through each major life area and redesign your expectations.

Be as grand and as free as you can, and then stretch some more. Let your inhibitions disappear. No one need ever read this. This is for you. Don't worry about being greedy.

1. **Body expectations**: If you were Tina, you might say, "I want the best body I can possibly have. I want to feel strong and fit and good about my body. I want to be in the best shape I can be. I will do whatever it takes to feel proud of my body. I want to push the limits on what I have done before. I will find a way to get a trainer so I can get the support and instruction I need to meet my goals. Nothing and nobody, especially me, is going to stop me. I've always wanted to learn how to ice-skate. I grew up in Southern California where nobody did that, at least no one I knew, and I'm going to live my dream."

2. **My action plan**: If you were Tina, you might say, "I'm going to talk to my friend Val. Her friend Jill teaches aerobics and is a personal fitness coach. I've only got a little money for this, but I am determined to find a way. I do have a lot of clothes I don't wear in the closet and I can sell some of those at the resale shop. I am determined, and I'm not going to let anything stop me. I will find a way. Other women have done this, in fact, Val is one of them. I'm going to take her for coffee and find out more about how she figured out how to feel good in her body.

   • Call Val and set up a coffee date.

   • Keep track of the tiniest bit of progress toward my goal of being totally fit in my self-esteem journal.

   • Ask Val to introduce me to Jill.

   • Call up every gym in town and see when they have free fitness days. Look at my schedule and make those freebies a top priority.

- Start asking people what they do for exercise and why they like it.

- Go to the library and pick out one book to read on physical fitness.

- Ask Jill and Val to recommend some exercise videos for me to try out.

- Put a time frame for each step in my action plan and monitor myself daily about what I have done to move toward my goal of being the most fit I can be.

- Write down every single thing I do toward feeling fit and strong in my body. I am going to take credit for the smallest step I take to feel good in my body."

Review your other goals and upgrade them. Choose one life area where you are willing to create and follow your action plan. Give yourself credit.

Exercise: Follow Your Dreams

You are unique in the world. There is no one like you, never has been, never will be. You have a life purpose—the thing you can do better than anyone else. Your life purpose can be elusive and slippery. You may have to become a private investigator to solve the mystery of your life purpose.

The purpose of this exercise is to help you widen your vision, sensitize your hearing, help you tune into the secret dreams that exist inside you.

1. Make a list of all the things you have ever wanted to be and do. Be expansive. Don't let reality stand in the way. Be as wild and crazy in your imaginings as you can. Allow yourself to consider the following pursuits and expand the list further: orchestra conductor, singer, writer, artist, sensualist, lion-tamer, circus performer, dancer, teacher, gypsy, newscaster, actress, playwright, entrepreneur, publisher, agent, acrobat, clown, comedienne.

2. Pick one direction to explore and construct an action plan. If you picked "actress," and you are fifty years old, don't let your age stop you. Let yourself explore the world of acting. Go to amateur and professional plays. See lots of movies.

Read books about acting and actors. Take a class at your local community college or university or acting studio.

3. Become an actress. Think like an actress. Look at how others construct a bit of theater on the bus or at work. Try out different ways to do the same old thing and have a new experience. Try a new grocery store and play the part, at least in your own mind, of the five-star chef putting together a dinner party for four. Buy flowers and arrange them while playing the role of the flower arranger for the most popular show on television.

4. Dress the part. Tie a scarf in an interesting new way; combine two colors that you never wear together.

5. Audition for a part in a production. Enjoy the experience of your own courage and tenacity.

Exercise: The Concorde

Become your own sorceress. Use the power of your unconscious mind to catapult you into magical transformation. Discover how to stop riding the bus and get right on the Concorde by completing this exercise.

Record the paragraphs that follow in your own voice on audiotape. Get in a comfortable chair and take a few deep breaths. Find the center of well-being deep inside you. Record the paragraphs with confidence and certainty. Speak with assurance, even though you may have to act "as if." Listen to the audiotape once a day for three weeks. At the end of three weeks write down your current expectations for all areas of your functioning, just as you did in the exercise earlier in this chapter. Compare your new expectations with the previous ones. You will be amazed at what can change in twenty-one days, using attention and intention to move you ahead.

Imagine that you are twelve years old and that you get to walk to the public swimming pool by yourself for the first time. You are incredibly excited. This is the first really big thing you've done on your own. The rest has been kid stuff. You pick out what you're going to wear to the pool, close the front door, and start walking. Your feet barely skim the ground. It feels like you're flying. You hear a bird trilling, the sky is pastel blue, the air is fresh. You float by a rose bush with deep crimson open blooms and inhale the rich sweet smell. The sun warms your back and neck and arms.

Now you are fourteen and you are allowed to take the bus to the library after school to do research for your history class. It is so cool. You get to ride the bus with your best friend and the two of you put on lipstick and it doesn't get much better than this.

Now you are sixteen and you have passed the driving test in the car, and you felt so nervous you didn't know if you'd pass out or fail the test. You got your driver's license. Now your mom has let you take the car for the first time by yourself, and you are going over to your best friend's house and the two of you are going to the mall for only a little while and it is so unbelievably cool.

Now you are twenty-nine and you have read *Consumer Reports* and you know exactly how to negotiate the best price for the car you decided was the perfect one for you. No sales person or manager is going to get you to pay one penny more than the *Consumer Reports* formula. You, a woman, have actually bought a car and negotiated the best deal possible.

Now you are thirty-three and you have been traveling to your district office about once a month. Getting on the plane is old hat now, the thrill is gone. Your boss told you yesterday that he wants you to fly first class, because you have been doing such a great job, and he is promoting you and wants you to travel twice a month. You get more money too. You are excited. You've never flown first class. You take a deep breath and enjoy the smell of plush leather in the forward cabin. There's plenty of room to spread out your reports, and you can work productively in this ambiance. Your ability to think and integrate seems to have been upgraded to first class also.

Now you are forty-one and your boss tells you there is another promotion for you, if you want it. You will be the international rep for your district. You won't have to travel more than twice a month, and your boss sweetens the deal and tells you that because of the company's need to get you there and back quickly, you're going to have to fly the Concorde. You feel a little anxious. What are you going to wear that will be appropriate? You reassure yourself that you deserve the Concorde experience because of the way you do your job. Also, you remember that a long time ago, you wondered what it would be like to fly the Concorde. Now you're going to find out.

You step into the plush stately cabin and notice the smell of espresso. You see the rich colors—red, purple, yellow—of the bouquet of fresh flowers at each sumptuous seat. The flight attendant takes your coat and asks if there's anything she can get for you. You sink into your seat and soak up the experience. You allow yourself to wonder about what's next.

CHAPTER 8

Working on People Skills, Not People-Pleasing

People skills give you the ability to know what you think and feel, to communicate your wants and needs clearly, and to negotiate compromises in ways that respect your integrity and the rights of others.

The issue of people skills, or assertiveness, is complex for most women. Some of us can be assertive in the workplace and yet have tremendous difficulty being assertive in personal relationships. Others among us can be assertive in our intimate relationships, but have debilitating anxiety about being assertive outside the home; people-pleasing is so ingrained that we can't return a damaged item to the store because we are worried about causing conflict and inconvenience to others.

Assertiveness has sometimes gotten bad press. Assertiveness has been confused with narcissistic self-centeredness and aggression. Appropriate people skills are consistent with compassion and respect for yourself and others.

Why Are Women Afraid to Be Assertive?

It is difficult for many of us to be assertive because we fear that if we express our deepest needs, wants, and desires, we will be seen as aggressive and not feminine. Remember that the script for women encourages us to be polite, genteel, and nice at all costs. We are supposed to resonate to others' needs, not our own. Many of us have deep primitive fears that if we express our real wants, needs, and opinions, our relationships will be damaged or lost. We have been trained to believe that being feminine means taking care of others and accommodating their needs.

Beware! Too much self-sacrifice can erode your self-esteem and render you unable to help yourself or others.

Many of us experience powerful and pervasive fears that if we really assert ourselves we will not be liked or loved or accepted—perhaps we will even be abandoned. We may not even be aware of how we limit ourselves and our relationships by not speaking up and acting to achieve what we know we deserve.

We sometimes don't use our own well-developed people skills and end up people-pleasing, instead. And yet, most of us will stand up for, and even insist on, the rights of someone else, a child, a family member, a friend—even a stranger.

This chapter helps you identify skills you already possess and use on behalf of others, to help yourself. We need to concentrate on strengthening people skills and leave people-pleasing behind.

Nancy's Story

Nancy was gorgeous: five-foot-nine, blond, and statuesque. She collapsed into a chair, barely controlling her sobs. "I thought it would be different after I retired and came out West. It's just so frustrating. At times I can't control the tears and I feel even more pathetic and helpless. I just can't figure out how to stop being a doormat. I raised my two kids, finally left my alcoholic husband after twenty-two years, and retired early to try to have a life of my own.

"I just can't figure out what the problem is. I think I'm a good person. I try to consider other people and I'm very responsible. This whole thing is just making me more and more depressed. Even though I moved out here to get a new start, I feel pretty much the way I did before I retired—and that was horrible. I have to do something to change how I feel. If I thought the rest of my life was going to be like this, I just couldn't take it."

Nancy grew up in a family where her feelings and strivings were not acknowledged. Her mother and father were rigid and emotionally unavailable. Nancy's father took refuge in long hours of overwork, and her mother cleaned house compulsively. Nancy was a bright, introverted only child, who survived the emotional wasteland of her family by creating a richly detailed inner landscape. Nancy's inner world was inhabited by a British nanny who was a fabulous cook, Merlin, a sorcerer, who provided magic carpets to anywhere, and a best friend named Penelope who was mischievous and daring.

Nancy's Technicolor inner world got her through the barrenness of her real existence. As a consequence, she had very little experience communicating with real people. She fell back on being superficially compliant, because that was how she had survived in her family of origin. It worked! Other people loved Nancy—they saw her as sensitive, warm, and caring.

Nancy, however, felt depressed and confused most of the time. She couldn't understand why the focus was always on the other persons' needs, never hers, in all her relationships.

Nancy suffered from not knowing how to be assertive. She was good at people-pleasing, but she had few people skills. She often didn't know how she felt, what she thought, or what she wanted. This made her unable to communicate her real feelings, needs, and thoughts to anyone else.

Nancy decided to take an assertiveness training class. Her world opened up. She learned how to identify her feelings, thoughts, and needs. She also learned the communication skills to get her message across to others. She was able to practice her skills in class and then take the skills out into her world of relationships.

"I'm just amazed. After some serious practice, I feel like I can do anything I want. I also made some friends in the class and we meet once a week to support each other at being more assertive. I'm not perfect, but I learned that I need to go forward and say what I want and need. Even if I don't get what I want every time, I've made my best effort, and I feel great about that."

Learning how to ask clearly for what you want greatly increases the probability that you will get it. In addition, the investment of time and energy in improving your people skills is a powerful message to you that you are worthwhile and important: this message, from you to you, builds your self-esteem.

Take credit for developing your people skills. Congratulate yourself for making the effort toward self-enhancement.

Exercise: Improving Your Assertiveness Skills

The purpose of this exercise is to help you quickly develop or polish your ability to communicate assertively.

1. Week One: Use your self-esteem Journal to record your daily goals and progress in developing more skills for assertive communication. Every day, write down one feeling, one thought or opinion, and one preference.

For example:

- Feelings: "I feel resentful when you don't help me get the children ready for bed." "I feel happy when you tell me something you like about me." "I feel sad when we don't spend special time together."

- Thoughts or Opinions: "I think men and women have a lot of the same fears and wishes about intimacy." "I think our weekly meetings would run more smoothly if we had a rotating chairperson."

- Preferences: "I would like it if you would help me get the kitchen straightened up after dinner." "I would like you to give me negative feedback about my work performance privately, rather than in a group meeting."

2. Week Two: Set a goal of communicating to someone else one thought, one feeling, and one preference every day. Record your daily goal and what you accomplished in your self-esteem journal.

Notice how much better you feel about yourself when you act in your own behalf, stating more clearly how you feel, what you think, and what you want. Congratulate yourself for every bit of time and effort you devote to developing your people skills.

Acknowledge that changing yourself is not easy and that you deserve praise for every step forward. Notice how your self-esteem improves as you communicate more clearly about your thoughts, feelings, and preferences.

Some situations may be more problematic for you. It may be easier to communicate your wants, feelings, and thoughts to a co-worker, and harder to communicate clearly with your boss.

Saying how you think and feel and what you want becomes easier and easier over time. After some practice, these skills become more automatic, consistently building and nourishing your self-esteem.

CHAPTER 9

Becoming the Parent You Always Wanted

Becoming the parent you always wanted allows you to give yourself what you missed as an infant and child. As described in chapter 2 on healthy selfishness, what we need from parents is love, attention, appropriate limits, consistency, and emotional attunement.

As children, we needed to be seen for who we were. We needed to get the message that we are intrinsically lovable. We needed support as we developed competencies. All of this we needed to get from our parents, and yet we may not feel that we received it.

You are now going to learn how to become the parent you always wanted.

Self-parenting is the ability to provide yourself with consistency, unconditional love, nurturing, appropriate limit-setting, emotional attunement, and realistic feedback—all the things that a good parent provides her child.

Talking to Yourself in Kind, Realistic, and Positive Ways

Clients often confess that they talk to themselves, and they often ask if this means they are crazy. Talking to yourself is not necessarily crazy. Most of us, crazy and not, talk to ourselves all the time. The truth is, the conversation you have with yourself is the most frequent and enduring conversation of your lifetime.

In this ongoing conversation with yourself, you give yourself hundreds of value-laden messages every day about your worthiness and your competence. You may be aware of some of the messages; others remain unconscious.

Most women engage in too much negative self-talk and not enough positive self-talk. If you were listening carefully, you might find yourself saying things like: "Boy, you really blew it with the boss today. You may be a short-timer. Better start thinking about looking for a new job." "What a klutz I am. I can't seem to do anything right." "These flabby thighs have got to go." "I went off my diet again—there must be something wrong with me to have so little willpower about what I eat."

Think about it. How often do you catch yourself saying, "Boy, I did a great job on that presentation today." "I am proud of being such a good friend." "I feel really good that I took the time to go on a twenty-minute walk today." "I ate a reasonable amount today and I am proud of that accomplishment." "Hooray! I actually paid the bills today instead of feeling anxious about it. Congratulations to me!"

Most of us engage in a lot of negative self-talk and little or no positive self-talk. We also direct critical feelings toward ourselves, especially anger, blame, and guilt.

Exercise: Increasing the Positive Things You Say to Yourself

The purpose of this exercise is to bring you into more awareness of how much you engage in negative self-talk and to increase the frequency of your positive self-talk. You are learning how to become your own parent by doing what good parents do—they absolutely gush over the tiniest little thing their infant or child does.

1. Bring your negative self-statements into awareness and decrease their frequency.

   • Every morning, tell yourself that you want to be in complete and full awareness of all the negative things you think and feel about yourself during the day. By beginning to be more sensitive to your own conversations with yourself, you will be able to identify the negative thoughts and feelings you direct toward yourself.

   • When you notice that you are feeling upset or depressed, review the reasons why you are upset or depressed. Often you will find that a major cause of feeling upset or depressed is negative talk or feelings directed toward yourself. Other times, feelings will just occur spontaneously, not caused by your self-talk. Sometimes your upset feelings will be a response to your situation. Being a more acute observer of your internal landscape will allow you to begin to control your thoughts when it is appropriate.

- When you notice that you have made a negative self-statement or directed a nasty feeling toward yourself, stop the process. Use the word "stop" or another word of your choosing to signal yourself to stop. You will probably be surprised at the barrage of critical messages you deliver to yourself.

- In your self-esteem journal, record at least one positive achievement a day. By doing this, you begin to plant positive seeds. These accomplishments can be small: the road to improved self-esteem is traveled by taking small steps. Allow yourself to take credit for successes that you might ordinarily ignore: getting to work on time; taking good care of your appearance, especially when you don't feel like it; speaking politely with a co-worker; going out of your way to be helpful to another person; doing the dishes when you don't feel like it; going to work when it would be easier to call in sick.

Give yourself detailed congratulations for accomplishing the smallest little thing. Life can be difficult and stressful. Making the effort to function reasonably well is deserving of acknowledgment and praise. Nothing is too small to honor. Be as kind to yourself as you would to a friend, your child, or a stranger.

Improving Your Support System

Research has indicated that one of the most important factors contributing to longevity is consistent caring relationships. Those with little or no close supportive human contact die significantly earlier than those people who have close supportive relationships with others. This is a powerful reason to begin a program of improving your support system.

There are lots of ways to improve your support system. Volunteer work puts you in contact with others who may share your interests. Taking a class allows you to share an experience over time with other people and the common experience gives you something to talk about. You can also enlarge your social network by letting others know that you are interested in finding more friends.

Showing a genuine interest in other people and really listening to others are probably the most important keys to building your support system.

Exercise: Increasing Your Support System

This exercise is designed to help you increase your support system so that you will feel more cared for, more secure, more loved and liked, more valued, more nurtured.

1. Research your community and find out how you can volunteer, take a class, or meet new people (art gallery openings, book club).

2. Make an action plan. Choose one of the activities you have identified that will increase your support system and start doing it. Be open to others, ask questions about them, listen attentively.

3. Take credit for every single thing you do to increase your support system. Write everything down in your self-esteem journal.

4. If the initial activity you choose is not to your liking, pick another one and follow through.

Compliment Others and Reap the Rewards

We all want and need acknowledgment and appreciation from others. Many women have grown up in families where their faults were pointed out and their accomplishments went unacknowledged. We may sometimes treat ourselves and others in this same negative way. For these reasons, we often come away from interactions with bosses, partners, friends, and children feeling unloved and unappreciated.

Clients are often touched when their therapist acknowledges a strength or comments positively about an accomplishment of the client. It is a shock and a surprise to the client—almost as though they don't deserve such good stuff.

It is sobering to realize that we are often defensively ready to ward off the next onslaught of anticipated critical feedback. Most of us stumble and fumble when we receive a compliment because we are not used to receiving credit for the positive things about us. When your boss says she wants to see you about something, you probably usually start reviewing all the possible imperfections in your job performance and preparing your defense. If your spouse says he needs to talk with you, you probably start compiling the list of possible gripes. This is a particularly ingrained pattern for many women; we are often highly attuned to the nuance of what others say and do, and we automatically assume that if someone is upset, we must have done something wrong.

Giving compliments (acknowledging the baby or child in a positive way) is a critical component of good parenting. In the following exercise, you will practice giving compliments to others, to help learn how to compliment yourself

Exercise: Giving Compliments in a Way That Accrues to You

The purpose of this exercise is to help you give to others and enjoy the benefits that come back to you.

Decide that you will begin a two-week program of compliment-giving. Make your goal to give one compliment a day to another person.

Compliments should always be genuine. Giving false compliments erodes your self-esteem. You can't feel good about giving a false compliment. Compliments don't need to be huge in order to have significant impact. Let people know when you like how they look, what they say, what they do. Compliment your children when they pick up their toys; compliment bus drivers for being courteous; compliment clerks for being helpful or pleasant; compliment your boss for taking an interest in the project you're working on.

We often neglect complimenting those we are closest to. Compliment your spouse when he does something helpful or endearing. Tell your friend how much you appreciate her being a good listener.

Avoid adding a critical qualifier that ruins the compliment you've just given: "I really like what you're wearing, but . . ." Following a compliment with a critical qualifier makes the recipient feel confused and resentful. Often we operate like this because we are uncomfortable giving and getting compliments; it makes us feel anxious. To give a compliment and then take it away causes the other person to feel manipulated, distrustful, or resentful.

Reap the rewards. Give one compliment a day for two weeks, keeping a record in your journal of all the compliments you give and of all the compliments you receive. Notice that the more genuine compliments you give, the more you receive. Giving compliments on a regular basis makes you feel good in the giving.

CHAPTER 10

How Crisis Makes Us Grow

Crisis is a natural part of life. We often associate crisis with the negative events in life: death, divorce, serious illness, loss of a job, or natural disaster. But it's not so simple. Crisis is often embedded in major transitions throughout life, even the ones we think of as positive. Birth is often a joyous celebration of new life and creation, and yet crisis (a time-limited state of emergency in which there is a critical turning point, for better or worse) is often a part of the birth process. Marriage, the joining of two who will support each other's separateness as well as their union, is often attended by more than one crisis. Divorce, which we frequently perceive as negative, can be very positive if the partners were not suited to one another. Divorce, as painful as it is for children, can sometimes free them from being held hostage in the war zone of their parents' relationship.

Crisis is a crucible of experience that tests your internal strengths and weaknesses. You can find yourself at your best or at your worst when there is a state of emergency in your life. Crisis carries within it a turning point, time-limited, which offers you the potential of positive growth, damage, or disaster. Crisis can result in loss and a spiral downward; it can sometimes be the beginning of the end (an alcoholic who is confronted by family and friends about her alcoholism, but refuses to do anything about the problem). Crisis can also lead to a magical, fantastic, mystical awakening or transforming experience that moves your life forward in an unexpected, wonderful way.

The relationship of self-esteem and crisis is complex. When you have good total self-esteem, you will have a better chance of using crisis to expand your competency and your feelings of worthiness. If you have low self-esteem, it may be more difficult for you to move through a crisis into a positive outcome.

On the other hand, if you have low self-esteem, there may be times in which you can, with the right tools, propel yourself through crisis and improve your total self-esteem. You may have lived in a damaging and destructive marriage which, over the years, has naturally eroded your self-esteem. When you finally find the courage to leave the battleground of your marriage, you will have improved your self-esteem significantly.

Using appropriate exercises from this book, you can help yourself increase your total self-esteem while living through a crisis. As you develop practical techniques to help you handle yourself in a crisis, you will find your self-esteem becoming more resilient.

Read the following stories about other women in crisis to see how self-esteem building techniques can help you get through a crisis in the most positive way

Kim's Story

Kim was ecstatic when she discovered she was pregnant. She and her husband had been trying for seven years to get pregnant and had been talking about adoption for the last year.

Pregnant, Kim was beside herself with joy and anticipation. She didn't tell anyone until after four months. She had miscarried before and wanted to be sure the pregnancy was viable before spreading the news. Kim was fortunate. She had a little morning sickness in the first trimester, but nothing debilitating. Her energy was good, she was able to do just about everything she had before she got pregnant.

Somewhere in the fourth month of her pregnancy, however, Kim noticed that she was feeling depressed. It was the changes in her body that were getting her down, she thought. Kim had always been proud of her slim, fit body, and she worked hard to keep it that way. She was used to looking good in her clothes and naked in the mirror. Now things were changing. Kim's waist had thickened, and her stomach had begun to pooch out a little. Her six-pack abs were a thing of the past.

Kim was in a bind. She was excited about the baby and depressed about the changes in her body. She felt more depressed as she gained more weight and saw her old body slipping away from her.

Kim sought therapy. After using some of the body-acceptance techniques described in chapter 3, Kim began to cope with her feelings about the changes in her body. She began to understand that she was far more than just her body. Kim was able to resolve her crisis in a positive, esteem-building way.

Jackie's Story

Jackie was beside herself with grief. She and her mother Rebecca had experienced a lot of ups and downs in their relationship. For two years, as Rebecca was dying of cancer, Jackie had been her mother's main caregiver. Although Jackie and her mother had made peace in their relationship, Jackie still, a year and a half after her mother's death, couldn't seem to shake depression. Every morning when Jackie woke, she had a second or two of feeling okay, and then the reality, "My mother is dead," hit her and she felt the deepest sadness and hopelessness she had ever known.

Friends finally prevailed upon Jackie to go to a psychiatrist to see if some medication could help her rise out of her abyss of excoriating pain. The psychiatrist prescribed an anti-depressant and also referred Jackie to a grief support group. Jackie felt heard and profoundly understood in the support group. Jackie also used some of the techniques described in this book to help her acknowledge her feelings more directly and fully, and to learn how to soothe her intense upset feelings, and get herself moving when she was mired in depression, hopelessness, and confusion. These techniques (see chapters 4 and 5) helped Jackie to pace herself through the grief, allowing her to have some small but increasing pleasure every day.

The intensity of Jackie's grief about her mother never left her completely. It did diminish in frequency and Jackie was able to feel better and better as time went on.

Robin's Story

Robin was a gifted child neurologist. She loved her work and her patients loved her. She was warm, likable, and gifted with a dynamite combination of an incisive scientific mind, a deep intuition about health and illness, and a sensitive bedside manner.

Robin's parents had held high expectations for their only child, but had been unable to provide her with empathy or emotional nurturing. Robin got most of her good feelings about herself through helping others.

In her mid-thirties, Robin started having joint pain and soreness. Her symptoms escalated rapidly. She was diagnosed with rheumatoid arthritis and embarked on a treatment regimen that made it sometimes necessary for her to reduce her workload. Because so much of Robin's self-esteem came from her work, she felt deflated, not able to provide her patients or herself with her usual dedication to work. Her self-esteem spiraled down and she blamed herself for somehow having caused her own medical problems. "Maybe if I hadn't worked so hard during residency, I wouldn't have gotten arthritis. Maybe if I had exercised more regularly and eaten real meals instead of grabbing food on the run, my immune system would be more resilient, more able to fight off these symptoms."

In therapy, Robin was able to silence her internal critic by using some of the techniques described in chapter 2 on healthy selfishness. In addition, she was able to begin to see that her worth was not just the superb job she did for her patients. Robin was gradually able to internalize the belief that she was worthy in and of herself, not only because she was an excellent physician.

Rachel's Story

Rachel was a doer. She was always moving, always in action. She had completed college, majoring in physical education, with a minor in English. Rachel was a natural athlete, and was a star on her college basketball team. Now, at twenty-five, Rachel was moving up in the ranks of the women's volleyball coaches at a prestigious university. Her job required her to be incredibly fit. At an away game, Rachel slipped on some water and ended up with a compound fracture of her right leg. The wound was slow to heal because Rachel tried to be as active as she usually was.

Her orthopedic surgeon finally laid down the law. She told Rachel that she was going to take her out of her work setting for six weeks, so that the fracture could heal properly. The surgeon referred Rachel to a physical therapist to supervise the healing process more closely. Rachel had always coped with her feelings by moving into action. When she couldn't be active in the old way, Rachel struggled with anxiety, depression, sadness, and hopelessness. She knew her leg would heal, but in order for that to happen, Rachel would have to learn how to deal with her feelings.

Rachel started keeping a journal of her daily experiences. She found that the writing helped her give voice to her helplessness, her hopelessness, her depression. As she continued her practice of daily writing, Rachel began to feel a little better. She had found a forum for her feelings and her own difficult experience. As the weeks went by, Rachel noticed that her writing time had increased. She also noticed that as her writing time had expanded, so had her relief.

Rachel decided to write about her own experience and put it in the form of a short story. One day as she was glancing through a women's magazine, she saw an invitation to enter a short-story contest. The prize was twenty-five hundred dollars and a trip to New York, home of the women's magazine. She entered the contest.

Rachel was astounded when she got a call three months later from the magazine. She had forgotten that she had submitted her story. The editor told Rachel that her story had won first prize in the contest. Rachel was excited. She went to New York and met with the editor, who was so impressed with Rachel's additional writing samples that she offered Rachel a spot as a short-story contributor. Rachel was delighted. The unexpected upside of her injury had led her to explore what turned out to be a great love of writing.

Lily's Story

Lily had worked as a computer consultant for fifteen years. The first few years were exhilarating, creating new programs, meeting new people. But the last few years, Lily was bored in her job. She plodded along, staying for the benefits and retirement plan.

Suddenly, disaster struck Lily's family. Lily's niece Erin had always been her favorite. Lily was shocked when she got the call from Erin's mother, telling her that Erin had just been court-ordered to a treatment program for drug rehabilitation. Even Erin's mom hadn't known that Erin was addicted to cocaine.

Erin's treatment program was located in Lily's city, so Erin's mom asked Lily if she would be willing to work with the drug-treatment staff and with Erin, to try to assist in Erin's recovery.

Lily was more than willing to help and make herself available to the treatment staff. She became closer to Erin during this process. When it was time for Erin to have an overnight away from the center, Lily and Erin were both anxious, fearful of Erin relapsing. The treatment staff had done their job well, and Erin had come a long way. The overnight visit went well. Erin made two slips and used again, but came back both times to her recovery protocol.

As she moved through the program with Erin, Lily noticed how connected she felt to some of the other adolescent girls in the treatment facility. After Erin had graduated from the program, the director asked Lily if she would be willing to do some volunteer work at the treatment center. Lily found that she loved working with the girls. She returned to school at night to pursue a degree in substance-abuse counseling, with a specialty in working with adolescents.

In the end, Lily's family crisis catapulted her out of a rut. Lily realized that by keeping her expectations low, she had kept herself down. Once she upgraded her expectations, her self-esteem and work life improved. Lily now works as an outpatient substance-abuse counselor with adolescent girls. She often muses how a family crisis led to her finding her life's work.

How to Crisis-Proof Yourself

Unavoidable crisis can and does happen to all of us. It makes sense for you to keep yourself in the best shape possible, in body, mind, and spirit, so that if a crisis develops, you will be able to deal with it. *Balance in yourself and your life is critical to how you handle crisis.*

Regular physical exercise allows you to feel fit and strong in your body. Physical exercise also helps your feel more strong and fit psychologically, as well as emotionally. Because the body-mind-spirit connection is interactive, you can make a change in your emotional state (reduce the intensity of anger, sadness, or depression, or increase the intensity of feeling good by remembering a pleasant event) and have a positive result in your physiology.

You know from earlier chapters that balance for women involves fighting the reflex of taking care of others at too great an expense to ourselves. You know that you have to scrupulously monitor how much care you give to yourself: treats, praise, play time, time to just stare into space, not doing anything. You also have to monitor your nutrition, whether you are eating a healthy diet rather than grabbing fast food on the run.

Take care of unfinished business in as timely a fashion as you can. It is horrible to have a friend or loved one become ill and die when there are massive loose ends in the relationship.

Have the intention to stay one hundred percent in the moment. This moment is all we have. The past is gone and the future is yet to come. Staying present in the moment is an art and a skill—a process that you need to come back to again and again. Use the techniques in the self-soothing section of chapter 5 to help you learn how to stay present in this moment. Focus on your breath and on breathing several times during the day. Focusing on your breath can bring you immediately into your body and into the present moment.

Use and reuse the self-esteem building techniques that are described earlier in this book. The techniques will help you build a stronger and more resilient self. Strong self-esteem is a sure way to help you be the best you can be, now and when crisis comes.

What to Do if You Are in Crisis Right Now

You may be reading this book having just lost someone you love—through death, separation, or divorce. Your child may have just left home. You may have been laid off at work. You may have been struggling with chronic illness or diagnosed with a serious health problem. You may feel anxious, depressed, hopeless, confused, or angry and frustrated.

If you are in a crisis right now, turn to chapter 5 and do one of the self-soothing exercises. If you are not significantly more calm, repeat the exercise or try another one.

Reach out for help to family or friends that you trust. Tell them specifically and directly how you are feeling and allow them to listen and help you. Call your family physician or consider talking to a mental health professional. If you feel suicidal, call the crisis line or go to the nearest emergency room.

Treat yourself with loving-kindness during this difficult time. In crisis, we sometimes feel so depleted and fragile that we feel like we are going to fall apart. Remember that feeling like you are going to fall apart doesn't mean that you will. Be tender and gentle. Baby yourself when you need to and be tough when that is called for. Give yourself credit for every single thing that you do to care for yourself and others during the crisis.

CHAPTER 11

The Future of Your Self-Esteem

What is the future of your self-esteem? The bad news is that you may have had enormous difficulties and struggles to get to this exact moment in your life. You may have not gotten your needs met adequately in infancy or childhood. You may have endured traumatic events—the early loss of a parent or sibling, not enough food, even sexual or physical abuse. You may not have been nurtured or supported enough by your parents. You may have been in a bad relationship or marriage. You may have had a physical disability or a learning difficulty; you may have lived with chronic or acute anxiety or depression. You may have had substance abuse or alcohol problems. You may not have the life history you would like.

The good news is that you are right here, right now, at the end of this book. In your situation, this may be the beginning or middle of your re-creation of yourself, and your deep resilient self-esteem.

Many women have endured horribly traumatic experiences and risen from the ashes of their pasts to become who they really are—special, unique, successful, worthy.

Each of us has a life purpose. Your life purpose is at the center of your essence as a person. It is the invisible and recognizable quality of your particular self that makes you different from anyone else in the world. Your life purpose may be hidden from your view and difficult to find. Your life purpose is the specific thing that you can do better than anyone else in the world.

Inside of you, deep inside of you, is your heart's desire. Your heart's desire is your secret wish or fantasy about what you would like to do most in the world. Your heart's desire is a key to your life purpose.

How do you find your heart's desire? You have to become a detective. You have to use your fabulous skills of intuition, your ability to integrate thinking and feeling, your curiosity, and the kind of determination that you use on behalf of others every day of the week. In order to find your heart's desire, your have to use all of yourself, and then some, on your own behalf. Not an easy task for most of us.

Ask and listen. Ask for help. Ask frequently. Ask those who have obvious passion for what they do. Ask the woman bus driver who's humming and singing while she drives. Ask the woman yoga instructor who is a hundred percent present as she teaches. Ask the woman family practice physician whose work is her passion. Ask how they found their paths to their heart's desire and life purpose. Ask for divine inspiration and assistance. Keep asking.

You have to listen to the whispers of eternity that travel through your being. Listen. Listen to your dreams. Look for clues and meaning in everyday experience. Listen to where you resonate, where you find your spark. Listen to what interests you, what you are curious about. Listen as though every millisecond of every minute is a source of important information for you about your life purpose. It is.

There are legions of writers who have been rejected. Some of them keep on going and in the process, find their life purpose and live their heart's desire. Jack Canfield, author of *Chicken Soup for the Soul,* was represented by a fabulous New York agent and endured fifty-two rejections from major publishers before he took his book on the road. You know the rest. Clarissa Pinkola Estes, Ph.D., who wrote *Women Who Run With the Wolves,* was turned down by legions of publishing houses. When the book was published, it flew off the shelves. Stephen King has said that he could wallpaper several houses with his rejection letters.

Failures pave the road to success.

Your means to fulfill your heart's desire, to find your life's purpose, is inside you, waiting to be discovered. It is a mysterious journey. You may think that your heart's desire is ludicrous or outlandish, foolish. Maybe you want to be a dancer and you're forty. Maybe you want to be an actress and you're seventy. Maybe you want to write another *Harry Potter* series and you're nineteen. Don't give up.

Your life's purpose is yours and yours alone, and there is only one available position to be filled. It cannot be filled by anyone but you.

Exercise: Project Yourself Into Your Future and Then Make It Happen

The purpose of this exercise is to help you experience exactly how you will feel when you have found your life purpose and you are living your dream. It is not necessary for you to know your life purpose in order for you to be able to successfully complete this exercise.

Put the following script on tape and listen to it at least once a day.

> *I am looking at myself after I have given voice to my heart's desire and discovered my life purpose. I am looking at myself living my life purpose. Time is immaterial, an hour, a day, six months, a decade. It doesn't matter. I am looking at myself from the outside. I can see myself clearly, but I am outside of myself.*
>
> *And now there is an explosion inside—only I can't hear it, but I feel it. And now I am myself, having and living my life purpose. I am comfortable inside my body. I open my eyes and the colors around me are rich and vibrant. I feel peaceful and completely at home with myself. It is as though I have finally come home. I feel completely connected to myself, from the tips of my toes to the top of my head. I am breathing deeply and evenly, without any effort at all. I am in the flow of being. I am completely myself.*
>
> *Something makes me want to laugh or smile—I don't know what it is. But I feel good. I feel completely and totally my full complete self. I feel connected to the world, to plants, to the sky, to the universe. I feel peaceful. I feel whole. I feel content. I feel complete. I feel.*

References

American Association of University Women. 1992. *How Schools Shortchange Girls*. Washington, D.C.: American Association of University Women.

Anand, M. 1989. *The Art of Sexual Ecstasy: The Path of Sacred Sexuality for Western Lovers*. Los Angeles: Jeremy P. Tarcher.

Bakan, D. 1966. *The Duality of Human Existence*. Chicago: Rand McNally.

Baumkind, D. 1968. Authoritarian vs. authoritative parental control. *Adolescence* 3:255–272.

Bednar, R., G. Wells, and S. Peterson. 1989. *Self-Esteem: Paradoxes and Innovations in Clinical Theory and Practice*. Washington, D. C.: APA.

Branden, N. 1994. *The Six Pillars of Self-Esteem*. New York: Bantam Books.

Briggs, D. 1970. *Your Child's Self-Esteem*. New York: Doubleday.

Broverman, I., S. Vogel, D. Broverman, F. Clarkson, and P. Rosenkrantz. 1972. Sex-role stereotypes: A current appraisal. *Journal of Social Issues* 28:59–78.

Burford, H., and L. Foley. 1996. Gender differences in preschoolers' sharing behavior. *Journal of Social Behavior and Personality* 11(5): 17–26.

Carter-Scott, C. 1998. *If Life Is a Game, These Are the Rules*. New York: Bantam Doubleday Dell Publishing Group.

Chopra, D. 1993. *Ageless Body, Timeless Mind: The Quantum Alternative to Growing Old*. New York: Harmony Books.

———. 1994. *The Seven Spiritual Laws of Success*. San Rafael, Calif.: Amber-Allen Publishing and New World Library.

————. 1996. "Journey to the Boundless" workshop, April 18–20, Los Angeles.

Clegg, E., and S. Swartz. 1997. *Goodbye Good Girl*. Oakland, Calif.: New Harbinger Publications.

Coopersmith, S. 1967. *The Antecedents of Self-Esteem*. San Francisco: Freeman and Company.

Cousens, G. 1986. *Spiritual Nutrition and the Rainbow Diet*. San Rafael, Calif.: Cassandra Press.

Eating Disorders Awareness and Prevention Center. 2000. Eating Disorders in the USA: Statistics in Context. http://www.edap.org /edinfo/stats.html.

Ekman, P. 1994. All emotions are basic. In *The Nature of Emotion: Fundamental Questions*, edited by P. Ekman and R. Davidson. New York: Oxford University Press.

Etaugh, C., and M. B. Liss. 1992. Home, school and playroom: Training grounds for adult gender roles. *Sex Roles* 26:129–147.

Fagot, B.I. 1977. Consequences of moderate cross gender behavior in preschool children. *Child Development* 48: 902–907.

Fagot, B. I., and G. R. Patterson. 1969. An in vivo analysis of reinforcing contingencies for sex role behaviors in the preschool. *Developmental Psychology* 1:563–568.

Friedan, B., 1963, 1984. *The Feminine Mystique*. New York: Dell Publishing.

————. 1997. *Beyond Gender: The New Politics of Work and Family*. Washington, D.C.: Woodrow Wilson Center Press.

Fredrickson, B. L., and T. A. Roberts. 1997. Objectification theory: An explanation for women's lived experience and mental health risks. *Psychology of Women Quarterly* 21:173–206.

Goleman, D. 1995. *Emotional Intelligence: Why It Can Matter More Than IQ*. New York: Bantam Books.

Golombok, S., and J. Rust. 1993. The measurement of gender role behavior in preschool children: A research note. *Child Psychology and Psychiatry* 34:805–811.

Gray, J. 1992. *Men Are from Mars, Women Are from Venus*. New York: HarperCollins Publishers.

Hardin, K. 1999. *The Gay and Lesbian Self-Esteem Book*. Oakland, Calif.: New Harbinger Publications.

Hartley, P. 1998. Eating disorders and health education. *Journal of Psychology Health and Medicine* 3:135–140.

Kaplan, L. J. 1991. *Female Perversions: The Temptations of Emma Bovary.* New York: Nan A. Talese/Doubleday.

Kelly, J. A., M. S. Caudill, S. Hathorn, and C. G. O'Brien. 1977. Socially undesirable sex correlated characteristics: Implications for androgyny and adjustment. *Journal of Consulting and Clinical Psychology.* 45:1185–1186.

Kindlon, D. and M. Thompson. 1999. *Raising Cain: Protecting the Emotional Life of Boys.* New York: Ballantine Publishing Company.

Lamb, M. E., and J. L. Roopnarine. 1979. Peer influences on sex-role development in preschoolers. *Child Development* SO:1219–1222.

Larsen, M. 1997. *How to Write a Book Proposal.* Cincinnati, Ohio: Writer's Digest Books.

Lazarus, R. S., and B. N. Lazarus. 1994. *Passion and Reason: Making Sense of Our Emotions.* Oxford: Oxford University Press.

Liss, M. B., ed. 1983. *Social and Cognitive Skills: Sex Roles and Children's Play.* New York: Academic Press.

Maccoby, E. E., and C. N. Jacklin. 1974. *The Psychology of Sex Differences.* Stanford: Stanford University Press.

Masterson, J. F. 1988. *The Search for the Real Self: Unmasking the Personality Disorders of Our Age.* New York: The Free Press.

Matlin, M. W. 1996. *The Psychology of Women.* New York: Harcourt Brace.

McKay, M., and P. Fanning. 2000. *Self-Esteem.* Oakland, Calif.: New Harbinger Publications.

Mehrabian, A. 1972. *Nonverbal Communication.* Chicago: Aldine-Atherton.

Mruk, C. 1995. *Self-Esteem: Research, Theory and Practice.* New York: Springer Publishing Company.

National Institute of Diabetes and Digestive and Kidney Diseases. 2000. Statistics Related to Overweight and Obesity. http://win@info.niddk.nih.gov.

Noll, S., and B. L. Fredrickson. 1998. A mediational model linking self-objectivation, body shame, and disordered eating. *Psychology of Women Quarterly* 22:623–636.

Parsons, T., and R. Bales. 1955. *Family, Socialization, and Interaction Process.* New York: The Free Press.

Pipher, M. 1994. *Reviving Ophelia: Saving the Selves of Adolescent Girls.* New York: Ballantine Books.

Rubin, T., F. Provenzano, and Z. Luria. 1974. The eye of the beholder: Parents' view of sex of newborns. *American Journal of Orthopsychiatry* 44:512–519.

Schwartz, B. 1996. *Diets Don't Work*. Houston: Breakthru Publications.

Sidorowicz, L., and G. Lunney. 1980. Baby x revisited. *Sex Roles* 6: 67–73.

Simon, D. 1999. *Return to Wholeness*. New York: John Wiley and Sons.

Stern, D. 1985. *The Interpersonal World of the Infant*. New York: Basic Books.

Strauss, R. 2000. Self-esteem related to childhood obesity. *The Brown University Child and Adolescent Behavior Letter 16* (March):3.

Wells, K. B., R. Sturm, C. D. Sherbourne, and L. S. Meredith. 1996. *Caring for Depression, RAND Study*. Cambridge: Harvard University Press.

Stephanie W. Dillon, Ph.D., is a clinical psychologist with twenty-five years of experience as a psychotherapist and teacher. Dr. Dillon appears frequently in the television, radio, and print media. She has produced self-esteem workshops for federal, state and local governments and for corporations, school districts, colleges, and universities. In addition, she is a consultant to corporations and school districts.

M. Christina Benson, M.D., is a psychiatrist and psychoanalyst in private practice in Los Angeles. She is affiliated with UCLA and has been involved in the supervision and education of medical students, psychiatric residents, and psychoanalytic trainees. Dr. Benson is a nationally known Tavistock trained consultant on group process and has contributed to a monthly column in the San Francisco Examiner.

Some Other
New Harbinger Titles

The Well-Ordered Office, Item 3856 $13.95

Talk to Me, Item 3317 $12.95

Romantic Intelligence, Item 3309 $15.95

Transformational Divorce, Item 3414 $13.95

The Rape Recovery Handbook, Item 3376 $15.95

Eating Mindfully, Item 3503 $13.95

Sex Talk, Item 2868 $12.95

Everyday Adventures for the Soul, Item 2981 $11.95

A Woman's Addiction Workbook, Item 2973 $18.95

The Daughter-In-Law's Survival Guide, Item 2817 $12.95

PMDD, Item 2833 $13.95

The Vulvodynia Survival Guide, Item 2914 $15.95

Love Tune-Ups, Item 2744 $10.95

The Deepest Blue, Item 2531 $13.95

The 50 Best Ways to Simplify Your Life, Item 2558 $11.95

Brave New You, Item 2590 $13.95

Loving Your Teenage Daughter, Item 2620 $14.95

The Hidden Feelings of Motherhood, Item 2485 $14.95

The Woman's Book of Sleep, Item 2418 $14.95

Pregnancy Stories, Item 2361 $14.95

The Women's Guide to Total Self-Esteem, Item 2418 $13.95

Thinking Pregnant, Item 2302 $13.95

The Conscious Bride, Item 2132 $12.95

Juicy Tomatoes, Item 2175 $13.95

Call **toll free, 1-800-748-6273,** or log on to our online bookstore at **www.newharbinger.com** to order. Have your Visa or Mastercard number ready. Or send a check for the titles you want to New Harbinger Publications, Inc., 5674 Shattuck Ave., Oakland, CA 94609. Include $4.50 for the first book and 75¢ for each additional book, to cover shipping and handling. (California residents please include appropriate sales tax.) Allow two to five weeks for delivery.

Prices subject to change without notice.